Heroic Faith

by

The Voice of the Martyrs

W PUBLISHING GROUP

www.wpublishinggroup.com

A Division of Thomas Nelson, Inc.
www.ThomasNelson.com

Published by W Publishing Group, a Division of Thomas Nelson, Inc., P.O. Box 141000,
Nashville, Tennessee 37214.

Unless otherwise noted, Scripture quotations are taken from the *Holy Bible: New International
Version,* NIV. Copyright © 1973, 1978, 1984 by International Bible Society. Used by permission
of Zondervan Publishing House. All rights reserved.

Scripture quotations noted *The Message* are from *The Message,* copyright © 1993, 1994, 1995 by
Eugene H. Peterson.

Library of Congress Cataloging-in-Publication Data

Heroic faith / by the Voice of the Martyrs.
    p. cm.
   ISBN 0-8499-4382-5
   1. Persecution. 2. Christian martyrs. I. Voice of the Martyrs
   (Organization)
BR1604.23 .H47 2002
272--dc21

                                 2002007542

Printed in the United States of America
02 03 04 05 06 07 LBM 9 8 7 6 5 4 3

*T*his book is dedicated to all those who
have gone before us,
who have consistently demonstrated
the qualities of *Heroic Faith,*
even in the face of extreme difficulties.
They have become our cloud of witnesses.
May we run the race well.

Contents

Heroic Faith

Unlike the average
card-carrying commitment
of many,
the faith of heroes
can't be neatly folded in a wallet
or buried in a purse.
Heroic faith
is more than casually hanging
a cross round your neck
or willingly wearing
a band of four initials
on your wrist.
The gist of heroic faith
is the way it flavors
whatever you find yourself
in the midst of.
It is the kind of faith
disciples of Jesus
are dying to claim.

BY GREG ASIMAKOUPOULOS

Acknowledgments

THE BOOK YOU HOLD IN your hand represents many hours of work, by many different people. All those involved hope these pages will fire your passion to serve our Savior.

Several people deserve recognition for their efforts on this project.

Thank you to Greg Asimakoupoulos, who was the primary writer. His many hours spent shaping this book to be true to our message and our persecuted family members are greatly appreciated.

I am grateful to Mark Sweeney and the entire team at W Publishing Group. I appreciate their partnership in telling the powerful stories of the persecuted church.

Greg Daniel worked diligently to make this a book that reaches the reader and communicates our passion to serve our brothers and sisters in restricted nations. Thank you, Greg.

Dave Veerman and his associates at Livingstone helped with writing and editing. Once again, they showed professionalism and passion, and I am grateful.

Thank you also to Steve Cleary and Todd Nettleton, who

shepherded this work into print on behalf of The Voice of the Martyrs. Many others also contributed thoughts and ideas in the writing process, helping to make the final product what it is.

Finally, I thank God for his blessings on our ministry and the special calling he has given us. This book is for his glory. I also thank the many brothers and sisters who are living examples of *Heroic Faith*, serving Christ in difficult circumstances around the world.

—TOM WHITE
USA Director, The Voice of the Martyrs

Introduction

Now faith is being sure of what we hope for and certain of what we do not see. This is what the ancients were commended for. (11:1–2)

All these people were still living by faith when they died. They did not receive the things promised; they only saw them and welcomed them from a distance. And they admitted that they were aliens and strangers on earth. People who say such things show that they are looking for a country of their own. If they had been thinking of the country they had left, they would have had opportunity to return. Instead, they were longing for a better country—a heavenly one. Therefore God is not ashamed to be called their God, for he has prepared a city for them. (11:13–16)

And what more shall I say? I do not have time to tell about Gideon, Barak, Samson, Jephthah, David, Samuel and the prophets, who through faith conquered kingdoms, administered justice, and gained what was promised; who shut the mouths of lions, quenched the fury of the flames, and escaped the edge of the sword; whose weakness was turned to strength; and who became powerful in battle and routed foreign armies. Women received back their dead, raised to life again. Others were tortured and refused to be released, so that they might gain a better resurrection. Some faced jeers and flogging, while still others were chained and put in prison. They were stoned; they were sawed in two; they were put to death by the sword. They went about in sheepskins and goatskins, destitute, persecuted and mistreated— the world was not worthy of them. They wandered in deserts and mountains, and in caves and holes in the ground. These were all commended for their faith, yet none of them received what had been promised. God had planned something better for us so that only together with us would they be made perfect. (11:32–40)

Therefore, since we are surrounded by such a great cloud of witnesses, let us throw off everything that hinders and the sin that so easily entangles, and let us run with perseverance the race marked out for us. Let us fix our eyes on Jesus, the author and perfecter of our faith, who for the joy set before him endured the cross, scorning its shame, and sat down at the right hand of the throne of God. Consider him who endured such opposition from sinful men, so that you will not grow weary and lose heart. (12:1–3)

SITTING IN AIR-CONDITIONED COMFORT, surrounded by evidence of "the good life" and breathing the fresh air of religious freedom, we can easily lose touch with many painful realities outside our country's borders. And reports of terrorism, persecution, torture, and other atrocities seem distant and only occasionally attract our attention. Engaged with family, church, and community concerns, we find it difficult to focus on anything beyond our busy schedules, especially events on the other side of the world that seem far removed from our daily concerns.

Then, without warning, terrible headlines invade our consciousness—war in the Middle East, tribal warfare in Africa, ethnic cleansing in Europe, terrorists' plots, Christians on trial—and we are brought face-to-face with evil and reality. When our awareness is heightened and we see the victims, our complacency quickly turns to grief, anger, and world awareness. And we gain a new appreciation for the survivors and rescuers, for the heroes of those conflicts.

Although news of international events may awaken us to a new sense of the heroic, a trip around the world and throughout history may do even more to awaken our senses. The world knows another kind of hero: the spiritual hero. For two thousand years, heroes of the faith have endured terrible suffering, simply for pledging their allegiance to Christ. They have chosen to willingly pay the costly price of commitment to the Lord rather than sell out in the name of cultural compromise.

The eleventh chapter of Hebrews gives us a handle on the heroes who comprise that great cloud of witnesses. They include Noah, Abraham and Sarah, Moses, Rahab, Gideon, Samuel, and David. And many others are not even named. The writer of this epistle calls attention to the heroic faith of those who conquered kingdoms (Joshua); those who shut the mouths of lions (Daniel); those who quenched the fury of the flames (Shadrach, Meshach, and Abednego); those who escaped the edge of the sword (Esther); those whose weakness was turned to strength (Simon Peter and Nicodemus); those women who received back their dead, raised to life again (Mary and Martha); those who were tortured and refused to be released (Stephen); those who faced jeers and flogging (Paul and Silas); and those who were chained and put in prison (Paul and John).

Still others are referenced who were barely footnotes in the pages of sacred history. These are the faithful thousands whose names are not mentioned in Scripture but who were stoned or sawed in half or run through with the emperor's sword, those who dressed in animals' skins by virtue of being homeless, poor, and persecuted.

Note what the writer to the Hebrews says about this company of heroes—"the world was not worthy of them." Isn't that great? These who were distinguished by their valor and faith were not recognized for who they truly were. Those who put them in chains or put them to death didn't have a clue. As far as the persecutors were concerned, the godly were not worthy of living. But in actuality, the world was not worthy and did nothing to deserve their presence.

Still, the list of heroes of the faith found in Hebrews 11 is far from exhaustive. Whereas they unquestionably had heroic faith, they are not the only ones we can point to who did. Obviously, Augustine of Hippo did. So did Bernard of Clairvaux. Add John Wycliffe to the list. And don't forget about Martin Luther, Isaac Watts, George Mueller, Amy Carmichael, and Oswald Chambers.

Erick and Evie Barendsen belong on that list. This American missionary couple lived out their faith in a humble home in Kabul, Afghanistan. Their desire was to be the presence of Jesus in an Islamic nation simply by serving people. Afghan Muslims and Christians alike came from many miles in search of the Barendsens. They knew they could receive personal support or medicine from them. But not everyone in Kabul appreciated this couple's mission, and opposition grew to their indirect evangelism.

When the Barendsens and their two children (ages five and three) returned to the States in 1980 for a brief furlough, friends and family seemed surprised as they heard Erick and Evie speak with excitement about returning to Kabul. "How can you go back? Won't it be dangerous?" people asked.

"I know of only one great danger," Evie answered. "The only danger is not to be in the center of God's will."

When the family of four returned to Afghanistan, Erick and Evie were attacked in their home and killed by switchblade-wielding Muslims. The thought of the Barendsens' home being a makeshift pharmacy and meeting place for Christians was more than the killers could handle. Despite the bloody invasion, two orphaned children are not all that were left behind. An underground church continued to grow.

Most likely, until now, you had never heard or read of Erick and Evie Barendsen. And the names Johannes Mantahari, Nijole Sadunaitae, Pastor Im, Jon Lugajanu, Linh Dao, and Nicolaie Moldavae probably seem totally foreign. Yet these men and women, members of the persecuted church, stand as powerful examples of ordinary Christians who distinguish themselves by their extraordinary faith. They are true heroes, and they help fill the bleachers of faith that Hebrews describes.

When you read through the forty verses of Hebrews 11 and you get to the first verse of Hebrews 12, what additional heroes do you think of? Who are the men and women whose personal influence or example have qualified them in your mind as those who deserve reserved seating in heaven's grandstand?

As you contemplate how you would answer that question, consider a couple of other questions. What distinguishes heroic faith from the plain vanilla kind? What qualities mark the lives of those you long to be like? In looking closely at hundreds of Christian martyrs and other persecuted believers, we found several distinguishing characteristics. If you were to conduct your own survey, you would find these same eight qualities.

1. *They are energized by an eternal perspective.* Individuals with heroic faith see beyond this world to the eternal realities. Rather

than live for the moment and for this world, they look to the next, knowing that this life is not all there is.

2. *They have an uncanny dependence on God.* This quality is evidenced primarily by a life bracketed by prayer. Those whose faith is of a heroic caliber talk to God as if they know him because they do. And because they believe he hears them, they are less anxious than most.

3. *They love the Word of God.* They love to read it, study it, and hear it read as well as preached. Not every person with a dog-eared Bible is a hero of the faith, but it is likely that all who are have well-worn copies of the Scripture.

4. *They are outrageously courageous.* When it comes to standing up for what they believe in, they aren't inclined to sit on their hands. These people possess a heroic boldness that flows out of their perspective of, total dependence on, and love for God's Word.

5. *They are living examples of what it means to endure.* Quitting is not a concept with which they are familiar. And because faith heroes view life as a long-distance race, speed is not nearly as important as stamina.

6. *They take obedience very seriously.* Pleasing God matters much more than accommodating people's unpredictable expectations. Heroic disciples delight in doing what they know God desires.

7. *They are unquestionably self-controlled.* Men and women who serve as heroic examples to the rest of us are not victims as much as they are victorious. They decide what the circumstances call for and act accordingly, even if it means voluntarily laying down their lives.

8. *They are marked quite simply by love.* Their eyes do not lie. Their countenance can warm the coldest room. People who have heroic faith are people who genuinely care for other people, and their actions prove it. Some might call it "faith in action."

Heroic Christians may appear to be larger than life, but they really aren't. Yet something about the quality of their faith inspires and motivates us to be more like them. By digesting the above-mentioned core values, they have discovered a growth potential that they might not otherwise have known.

This book attempts to examine these eight qualities in some detail. Each chapter will illustrate one of the eight by looking at heroes of the faith. We will pay particular attention to those within the persecuted church whose stories both inspire and challenge. People like Sharaz, a Bible college student in Pakistan.

Ever since Sharaz had embraced Christ's extended love, he couldn't keep it to himself. He just had to talk about it at home, in the Bible school he attended, and in the factory where he worked. His heart had been so transformed with love and forgiveness that he wanted everyone he knew to have the same experience.

While going about his job at the factory to support his parents and three sisters, Sharaz got into a discussion with some Muslim coworkers about his newfound faith. What began as a calm exchange of ideas escalated into a heated argument. It was the last time anyone saw Sharaz alive.

A week later, his bloody body was left in a heap at the front door of the church in Lahore, Pakistan, where Sharaz worshiped.

Attached to his corpse was a message with only four words: "Stop preaching to Muslims."

Yes, Sharaz had known the risks of witnessing to those who follow Islam. He was aware of many Pakistani Christians who had been killed for sharing their faith. He knew of others who had been charged with blasphemy and imprisoned. But Sharaz had a cause. As a new creation in Christ, he was on a mission. He couldn't keep God's love to himself.

Neither could his fellow church members. When they recovered his body, they reverently gave it a decent burial. But they threw the note away. There was no way they would let four little words stop them from standing up for the truth for which Sharaz had laid down his life.

As you contemplate the legacy of faith heroes, picture them as the writer to the Hebrews does. The saints of the ages are seated in a celestial stadium. Much like the Olympian athletes who have competed in their events and await the closing ceremonies while perched in their place of honor in the grandstands, those who have gone before us encircle the track.

Unlike the athletes at the Olympic games, however, those who have finished their competitions have not stood on a podium for the medals ceremony. According to Hebrews 11:39–40, they are waiting for those of us who have yet to complete our race.

So these whose lives have modeled the faith we desire now witness our progress and cheer us on.

CHAPTER 1

Eternal Perspective

Focused on the Future

With a vision for what's in store,
heroes look at more
than just the present reality.
They focus on the future.
They have eyes to see what others can't
and claim the view they can.
While some may boast 20/20 hindsight,
heroes are not inclined to find meaning
gazing into rearview mirrors.
They rather find their point of reference
beyond the windshield of today.
That is to say,
in glancing at their passports
they're reminded this world is not their home.
Heroes, you see, are farsighted.

BY GREG ASIMAKOUPOULOS

"WE ARE NOT GOING to torture you anymore!"

Paulus wondered what the Soviet officer's words meant. He had been beaten and abused for several hours, and all for the crime of following Jesus Christ. Challenging the pain that bent him over, Paulus sat up to hear the soldier continue.

"No, we aren't going to torture you anymore. We are sending you to Siberia where the snow never melts. It is a place of great suffering." And with mocking laughter the officer added, "You and your family will fit in very well."

Paulus's response surprised the uniformed Soviet. He smiled and told his captor, "The whole earth belongs to my Father, Captain. Wherever you send me I will be on my Father's earth."

The captain mocked Paulus's optimism. "We will take away all you own. We will put a bullet between your eyes."

Paulus, with a broad grin, responded, "You will need a high ladder, Captain. My treasures are stored up in heaven. If you take away my life in this world, my real life of joy and beauty will begin. I'm not afraid of being killed."

The Christian's confidence angered the captain. He grabbed Paulus by his tattered prison shirt and screamed in his face, "Then we will not kill you. We will keep you locked alone in a cell and allow no one to come and see you!"

Paulus continued to smile as he humbly challenged the officer's intention, "You cannot do that, sir. You see, I have a Friend who can pass through locked doors and iron bars. No one, not even you, can separate me from the love of Christ."

As the Soviet captain promised, the immediate future for Paulus and his family meant resettlement in Siberia. Not the easiest place to be sent. In the Soviet Union during the 1980s, Siberia meant more than severe weather and poverty. Historically, it was a synonym for cruel punishment or even death.

But neither Paulus nor his wife was tempted to back away from their verbalized trust in the Lord. They had placed their confidence in Jesus. They knew their ultimate future was a destination no one could take from them. Because of their eternal perspective, they had a spiritual antenna that allowed them to pick up a frequency their Soviet interrogators were oblivious to. It was a signal that would be just as strong in Siberia as any other place.

A Picture of Faith at a Football Game

On a warm autumn afternoon in 1982, the Spartans of Michigan State were invading Badger Stadium in Madison, Wisconsin. The emotion was electric. The cheers were deafening. But to a young man attending his first Big 10 football game, something about the experience didn't make sense. Michigan State was clobbering the home team; yet, when the visitors completed a long pass or ran for a touchdown, Wisconsin fans cheered with all their might. It was strange. Although their team was being trounced, the home crowd responded as if they were winning.

Midway through the first quarter, the curious neophyte figured out what was going on. As it so happened, on that very day eighty miles away, the Milwaukee Brewers were hosting the St. Louis Cardinals in game four of the World Series. Football fans in Badger Stadium were listening on portable radios as the Brewers were soundly defeating the Cardinals. The cheers had nothing to do with the action on the gridiron; they were related to a reality no one could see.

Ben Patterson, the chaplain at Westmont College, says that hope is the ability to hear the music of the future. I like that. Those who have a heroic faith hear what others cannot—they march to a different drum. Like Paulus and his wife and children, they allow their knowledge of what awaits them to calm their troubled and tired souls. Hope in heaven becomes a soothing melody that lifts the anxious heart. Those with this kind of faith are like the Wisconsin fans. They let a long-distance reality dictate their emotions.

But Patterson says there's more. If hope is the ability to hear the music of the future, then faith, he adds, is dancing to it. In other words, faith results in taking action on what you know to be true, even when others aren't aware of the truth.

Those with an eternal perspective know the truth—that this life is not all there is—and they live that truth. Though burdened and beaten, they live with hope and joy. With antennas tuned to God's frequency, they hear his strong message and live accordingly.

Struggles and pain can cloud our vision, causing us to lose perspective. That's when we're tempted to give up or give in. We must remember that when we lose in this world, when we are deserted and persecuted because of our faith, we win with the Lord.

"Those who are with Jesus in suffering hear this music to which other men are deaf. They dance and do not care if they are considered insane."

Stop for a moment and check your perspective. Where are you looking? To whom are you listening?

In his remarkable little book *Victorious Faith,* Richard Wurmbrand resonates with Patterson. He writes: "There was once a fiddler who played so beautifully that everybody danced. A deaf man who could not hear the music considered them all insane. Those who are with Jesus in suffering hear this music to which other men are deaf. They dance and do not care if they are considered insane" (Bartlesville, OK: Living Sacrifice Book Company, 1979, p. 62).

What's the Therefore There For?

Can't you see Paulus and his wife waltzing their way to Siberia? More than just hearing the music of heaven in their heads, their faith allowed their feet to "hear" it as well. Their captors and persecutors thought them insane, but what else could they think? Those without Christ are deaf to the music of heaven.

That's exactly the image the writer to the Hebrews painted

when he defined *faith*. The very first verse of chapter 11 asserts that faith is being sure of what we hope for and certain of what we do not see. Or as Eugene Peterson phrases that verse in *The Message*, "The fundamental fact of existence is that this trust in God, this faith, is the firm foundation under everything that makes life worth living. It's our handle on what we can't see. The act of faith is what distinguished our ancestors, set them above the crowd."

We come from a long line of "God-trusters." Our spiritual ancestors consistently took their cues from a future that was only hinted at. Their ability to anticipate what they could not see distinguished them as people of faith. But it was their determination to factor the promises of eternity into their daily decisions that qualified them as heroic.

Those listed in Hebrews 11 actually acted as if the future were here even though they were only able to visualize ultimate exoneration, eventual rewards, guaranteed victory, and complete salvation in their heads. ("All these people were still living by faith when they died. They did not receive the things promised; they only saw them and welcomed them from a distance"—v. 13; "He persevered because he saw him who is invisible"—v. 27.) Those heroic men and women traded in the currency of heaven even though the rest of the world considered their certificates of deposit to be "funny money."

What was true of those whose portraits are hung in the Hebrews gallery of the faithful is also true of Jesus. Most everybody knows that the chapter divisions in the Bible were not inspired. They are simply mileposts in the text that ancient editors inserted in an attempt to break up the visual journey of the reader. It's unfortunate that Hebrews chapter 12 begins where it does. For one thing, look at how the chapter begins: "Therefore, since we are surrounded . . ." The way the verse begins demands that we know what has preceded it. To fully appreciate the flow of the text, we should read the entirety of chapter 11 and then carry on without stopping through the third verse of chapter 12. It is only when we have seen the multitude of these spiritual marathoners—it is only when we have had an opportunity to hear the trample of their footsteps and the labored breathing of their runner's pant—that we can fully appreciate the "therefore" when we get there.

In such a reading, clearly Jesus is the zenith of those who have been listed as examples of faith. He is the last of those named. We are called to be mindful of those faith heroes who have completed their marathon and are seated in the stands, but we are to fix our eyes on Jesus as the model of heroic faith. Then did you notice what the writer did? The same thing he did in the eleventh chapter. He added a little editorial comment that explains why Jesus' behavior is an example of faith.

We are told that our Lord maintained his momentum of obedience despite a myriad of obstacles. We are also told how he was able to do that. It was because of his eternal perspective: ". . . who for the joy set before him endured the cross, scorning its shame" (12:2). In other words, the Savior used the currency of eternity to pay our debt of salvation, a debt that cost him his life.

He factored the future into his present decisions and drew on what was not yet an earthly reality to embrace the reality that was.

A Vision Motivated by an Invisible Force

That's not the first time we see Jesus being influenced by his eternal perspective. The night before he was crucified, knowing full well what was in store, the Savior disregarded the human fear in his pounding heart and demonstrated heroic faith. And once again Jesus borrowed from the bank account of eternity to pay the costly price of humility. In the thirteenth chapter of his gospel, John provides a window into the upper room.

Jesus and the disciples were gathered to celebrate the Passover meal one last time. In the midst of the meal, the Lord wanted to take advantage of a teachable moment and model the lifestyle he was calling his colleagues to own. In that no servants were present to wash the filthy feet of the disciples (and since none of the Twelve had offered to play that role), Jesus himself took on the responsibility. Taking a towel and a clay-baked basin, Jesus went from friend to friend bending down to wash their feet.

When you stop and think about it, the degree to which Jesus stooped to demonstrate selfless devotion was unthinkable. It was the height of presumption. It was the depth of impropriety. God himself was on his knees doing what was necessary no matter how degrading. It was a preview of what would occur within the next twenty-four hours.

But John gives us a clue as to how Jesus closeted his divine prerogatives and did the hard thing. In John 13:3−4 we read, "Jesus knew that the Father had put all things under his power, and that he had come from God and was returning to God; so he got up from the meal, took off his outer clothing, and wrapped a towel around his waist."

Jesus was motivated to serve by what he saw beyond the horizon of this life. He could see the glory that awaited him across a cosmic border crossing. And because he could, he was willing to endure the humiliation, rejection, injustice, and brutal death that marked his earthly life. He knew he was merely passing through.

Jesus' awareness of eternity translated into an observable detachment from the values and demands of things on earth. Seeing what was just ahead, he willingly claimed the identity of a sojourner. He was not a citizen of this country. He knew he was a resident alien. He willingly resisted any attempt to become naturalized. And those who would submit to his Lordship are called to do the same.

Those who live with an eternal perspective keep their eyes on Christ. Seeing how Jesus lived—his choices, goals, and actions—helps us realize what is truly important and shows us what to do. Daily, other values and concerns compete for our attention. But when we turn and look that way and accept the world's values, we lose our perspective and lose our way. Consider, for example, the person who ruins his health to gain wealth, the woman who sacrifices her family in order to move up the corporate ladder, or the man who turns his back on twenty-five years of marriage for a fling with a younger woman. Believers are not immune—many have crashed and burned in the Christian life.

Take another perspective check: What values compete for your attention? When are you most tempted to take your eyes off Christ?

This World Is Not Our Home

Getting back to Hebrews 11, the chronicler of faith's hall of fame refers to the fact that all those who were motivated by what was still to come "admitted that they were aliens and strangers on earth" (11:13). They recognized that no matter how tempted they might be to settle down and unpack their suitcases, terminating the trip would be a terrible mistake. For the Christian, it is always premature to give up our tourist visas and become citizens of this world.

Convicted in a Lithuanian court, Nijole Sadunaitae awaited her sentencing. Her only crime was being a Christian in a Communist country. The judge offered Nijole a chance to speak, fully expecting her to plead for mercy. Instead, Nijole smiled as she said, "This is the happiest day of my life. I am on trial for the cause of truth and love toward men. I have an enviable fate, a glorious destiny. My condemnation here in this courtroom will be my ultimate triumph."

If we're honest, we have to admit we don't see quite as many people en route to heaven as we once did. More and more believers are trading in their sojourner tents in order to pour permanent concrete foundations. The cause is a condition that some observers of contemporary Christianity call "identity dementia." An increasing number of Christians have forgotten that people of heroic faith are by definition "aliens and strangers."

In her book *Soul Alert* (Carol Stream, IL: Mainstay Church Resources, 2002), Karen Burton Mains describes what occurs when citizens of the Kingdom of Heaven fail to consult their passport. Behaviorally, there is little difference between evangelical Christians and the rest of society. Christians spend seven times as many hours on entertainment as they do on spiritual activities. Less than a third of all young people raised in the church continue to attend worship once they leave home. In a nationwide survey conducted among born-again adults by the Barna Research Group, none of the individuals interviewed said that the single, most important goal of their life was to be a committed follower of Jesus Christ.

Mains writes, "This travel across life is not a pleasure cruise for the Christian. The soul of the church in contemporary western culture is in danger. We are allowing ourselves to be assimilated. There is little essential difference between us and the society that surrounds us. In fact, we long to be like the world. . . . While traversing this foreign culture, a thieving enemy is pinching our heavenly papers, and we are in danger of losing our distinctive identities as strangers and aliens in the world" (p. xvii).

"We are allowing ourselves to be assimilated. There is little essential difference between us and the society that surrounds us."

It's easy to see how this happens. The world's temptations pull and entice, offering pleasure, power, and prestige. So, like Esau, we sell our birthright for a bowl of stew, trading the future for the present (Genesis 25:29–34).

One of the reasons we may be inclined to lose our eternal focus may be a vision problem. How many sermons on heaven can you recall hearing in the past twelve months? If your church is like most, you probably haven't heard any. That is, unless you count funeral meditations. Those who communicate God's Word from the pulpit are not casting the vision of eternity. In an attempt to capture the imagination and interest of "seekers," preachers tend to deal with issues of the "here and now" as opposed to the "there and later." Problem-solving messages are aimed at touching felt needs within the congregation—pastors are bending over backward to articulate what the "abundant life" that Jesus came to bring looks like in our culture and generation. But in the process they are losing their balance and are falling prey to the appetite of those demanding instant gratification. A theology that points to heaven as the goal of our salvation is hard to detect.

Jon Lugajanu, a young believer in Eastern Europe, had been arrested and imprisoned for being a Christian. Returning to his cell after the court hearing to determine his sentence, other prisoners asked him what happened. Jon answered, "It was just like the day the angel visited Mary, the mother of Jesus. Here she was, a godly young woman sitting alone in meditation, when a radiant angel of God told her the incredible news. She would carry the Son of God in her womb."

Wondering how Jon's words would relate to his court appearance, the prisoners listened closely. Jon continued to tell the story of Jesus and to clearly present the gospel. He concluded by saying, "Mary knew once she was in heaven, she would be with Jesus again and experience eternal joy."

Puzzled, the prisoners reminded Jon that they had asked him what had happened *in court.*

Jon, his face shining, replied, "I was given the death penalty. Isn't that beautiful news?"

Jon realized that the news the angel delivered to Mary was just as bittersweet—after Jesus had suffered, heaven would be filled with rejoicing. Like Mary, Jon joyfully anticipated his eternal life in Jesus' presence. Jon could share his faith boldly and joyfully because of his eternal perspective.

Those who have an eternal perspective are not at home in the world. So if you're feeling comfortable, complacent, and cautious—at home here—perhaps your focus has changed. Check your perspective.

A Dress Rehearsal for What Is to Come

Pick up a hymnal from fifty years ago and look in the index for lyrics that celebrate the Christian's hope in the life to come. I think you'll be amazed. And if you go back even further, you'll find evidence of all kinds of hymnody that our forefathers and mothers held on to as handles of hope in the life to come.

Olga Watland was one such woman. Born near the turn of the twentieth century, she lived a very sheltered life. She was forced to quit school in the fourth grade to help on the family farm. Once married, she never worked outside the home. She never learned to drive. She rarely traveled far from home. But this uneducated woman with a simple faith had a personal relationship with Jesus that all who knew her admired. And she did raise three children, a son and two daughters. Each one benefited from the godly example they observed in their mother. Each of Olga's children went into the pastoral ministry.

In addition to her quiet, consistent faith, Olga Watland was also known for her fixation on heaven. While family constraints prevented her from continuing her formal education, this grandmother of eight taught herself how to play the electric organ, guitar, and harmonica. Her grandchildren have a myriad of childhood memories of Nana Watland entertaining them with spontaneous concerts.

Because of Olga's conviction that experiences in this life are only dress rehearsal for what is to come (and no doubt because of longings she had to be reunited with her parents and siblings who had died in childhood), most of her songs were about heaven.

One song in particular dated back to the early twentieth century, about the time blimps like the ill-fated *Hindenburg* could be seen ferrying people overhead like aerial boats. It went like this: *"I have good news to bring and this is why I sing and my joy with you I'll share. I'm going to take a trip in that old gospel ship and go a sailing through the air. Oh, I can scarcely wait. I know I'll not be late, for I'll spend the time in prayer. And when my ship comes in, I'll leave this land of sin and go a sailing through the air."*

Another one of Olga's unorthodox songs with a celestial focus chronicled the pain of a young family who lost their wife and mother to a premature death. It recalls the days before direct-dial telephones, when an operator ("Central") had to place one's call. *"Hello, Central, give me heaven for my mother's there. You can find*

her with the angels on the golden stars. She'll be glad to know I'm
calling. Tell her, won't you please. For I surely want to tell her we're
so lonely here. Telephone to glory, O what joy divine . . ."

Chances are, you never sang one of Olga Watland's songs in
the church you grew up in. But you likely did sing hymns such
as, "When We All Get to Heaven," "Beyond the Sunset," "This
World Is Not My Home," "He the Pearly Gates Will Open,"
"Shall We Gather at the River," and "Face to Face with God My
Savior." And as you stood to sing those great old lyrics, something within you visualized a wonderful reunion of all the saints
of all the ages. As you sang about heaven as a child, quite possibly your little mind did its best to wrap itself around the reality
that Christians are always looking beyond the present circumstances because the best is still to come.

A Child Shall Lead Us

On October 28, 2001, four-year-old Kinza al-Atta witnessed the
brutal murder of her pastor father, Emmanuel al-Atta. She says
she saw her daddy give one last loving glance into her big brown
eyes before he fell to the ground and "went to sleep." One
moment he was praising God from his pulpit, and the next he
was target practice for Islamic terrorists who entered the small
church firing their guns.

It's a given that Emmanuel's little daughter had never heard
the lyrics of Olga Watland's old-fashioned songs. But there is no
doubt Kinza al-Atta understood in her own childlike way the
reality of eternity. When asked the whereabouts of her daddy,

little Kinza said, "He's in heaven with Jesus." It's a theology lesson she learned by "singing" the songs of the suffering church firsthand.

Ecclesiastes 3:11 says that God has "set eternity in the hearts of men." So it is not far-fetched to think that a four-year-old could grab hold of the reality of what is beyond our reach and out of view. Solomon's words would imply that from the very beginning of our lives we have knowledge of eternity.

In her own limited experience of life, Kinza is aware that God is in control. Though still brokenhearted, she believes what her mommy tells her about her heavenly Father. That he is at work in her little life in spite of the suffering. That his ultimate plan involves far more than our happiness in this life. That he will give her the power to persevere through all the hardship of growing up without a daddy. That she will become a stronger Christian and will receive an eternal reward.

Kinza and her family are now receiving financial assistance through The Voice of the Martyrs' Families of Martyrs Fund. This will help Kinza and her family, despite the enormous financial burden that began when Islamic terrorists gunned down her daddy on that tragic October Sunday morning.

Heroic faith is not only the possession of those wrinkled by years. It is modeled by believers of all ages who look beyond the present circumstances to what is still to come.

Heroic faith is not only the possession of those wrinkled by years. It is modeled by believers of all ages who look beyond the present circumstances to what is still to come. Children who have lost parents to death or imprisonment find that the seed of eternity God planted in their hearts at birth germinates and grows at will. Teenagers who have witnessed a classmate's life snuffed out by a tragic accident find themselves looking at life beyond today with uncanny vision. A middle-aged businessman released by his employer because of company cutbacks is forced to come to terms with the security this life promises but is incapable of delivering. A young mother paralyzed for the rest of her life by a freak skiing accident reads the verse about "a new heaven and a new earth" with greater interest. In each case, faith that embraces the eternal dimension of one's relationship with the Lord distinguishes itself as heroic. It is a faith that anticipates what still awaits.

Though he was being burned at the stake at the order of Spanish authorities during the Inquisition, Antonio Herrezuelo's pain was in his spirit. He realized that his wife had renounced her faith in Christ to escape a similar death. Antonio could have also saved his life and been sentenced to prison like his wife. Then, perhaps, he would have someday been pardoned and been reunited with her.

But he would not recant. His last words, before the soldiers gagged him, were pleas to his wife. "Please return to Christ and be forgiven. We will be united together in heaven. Please return!" he yelled to her. With no earthly hope of reunion, he wanted to be with her in eternity.

After Antonio's death, Mrs. Herrezuelo was returned to the prison to serve her life sentence. For eight years she wrestled with

God and her own spirit. She could find no peace about her fateful decision.

Finally, she publicly returned to faith in Christ, recanting her previous denial even as the sixteenth-century Inquisitors threatened her. A judge gave her a new sentence, this time to death at the stake.

She accepted her fate eagerly because she finally was at peace. Mrs. Herrezuelo knew that her first words to Antonio would be of her return to the faith.

One of the lessons here is that to build an eternal perspective, we should involve ourselves with others who have one. They will model for us what it means to focus on Christ and his promises. Do you regularly fellowship with people of eternal perspective? Out of this fellowship, we can draw strength.

So how's your perspective? Do you see that this life is not all there is? Do you keep your eyes on Christ? Do you look forward to your heavenly home? If not, you need a prescription.

A Prescription to Correct Our Nearsighted Vision

Jesus said that a person's heart would be where that person had his or her treasure (Matthew 6:21). One way to gain a heavenly point of view, therefore, would be to store up "treasures in heaven" (Matthew 6:20). Visit a hospital or an elderly care facility where people are sick and dying. Spend time talking to and praying with the men and women there. That will help you think of eternity and keep your life in perspective.

■ What painful experiences (discouragement, frustration, persecution, depression, or suffering) have threatened to cloud your spiritual sight? Spend time talking with God about those issues, and ask him to help you see life from his point of view.

■ What kinds of lifestyle choices and values do you think mark people who approach this life as if it were all there is? How does your life compare? What evidence do you see that you have lost a godly perspective? What changes should you make to keep your eyes on Christ?

■ The Bible, God's Word, tells the truth about life and the life to come. The only way to gain a God's-eye point of view on life is to know what he says. How much time do you spend reading the Bible each week? Choose a Gospel and work your way through it, noting what Jesus taught about his kingdom and eternal life.

■ When did you last have a serious discussion with someone about heaven? How does knowing that heaven awaits you give you hope? With whom can you share your future vision?

CHAPTER 2

Dependence on God

Declaration of Dependence

While others try to make things happen,
heroes trust in what God wills.
They must.
They've signed a declaration of dependence
on the parchment of their hearts.
In prayer, they pledge their allegiance
to what God has planned.
Dropping to their knees,
heroes securely hold on
to what he has promised.
It is this posture of faith
that allows them to lean on God
and listen for his voice.
If you'd ask them why
they commune with the Lord,
they'd say they have no choice.

BY GREG ASIMAKOUPOULOS

JUST TWO YEARS AGO, eighteen-year-old Johannes Mantahari was living in a small village on Halmahera Island in Indonesia. One night he was suddenly awakened at 3 A.M. and told that a mob of Laskar Jihad troops had amassed nearby and was heading for his village. Johannes attempted to flee but was caught by about twenty of the radical Muslim warriors.

Five of them pinned him down to the ground. Ten of them surrounded him so he could not escape, and five stood above him with samurai swords, ready to attack. Johannes was asked if he wanted to become a Muslim. He said no. His attackers said they would kill him if he refused to convert. Assured of his salvation, Johannes said he was prepared to die.

The Laskar Jihad troops struck Johannes's left temple with the razor-sharp tip of the samurai sword then sliced into his left shoulder and forearm. Another one of the invading Muslims took the sword and slashed the back of Johannes's neck. To finish him off, they slashed Johannes again with a samurai sword, this time across the back and legs. Then the warriors covered Johannes's lacerated body with banana leaves and attempted to light them on fire to incinerate his body. The leaves were too green and would not light. Then the Jihad troops left Johannes for dead.

Johannes lay bleeding as the Laskar Jihad warriors fled into the jungle. With his last few breaths of life, Johannes cried out to God for help. Suddenly, he felt enough strength in his arms and legs to remove the banana leaves and escape into the jungle. Johannes hid in a cave until it was safe to come out. He stumbled through the jungle for eight days, crying out for help. He found no one and finally collapsed from exhaustion, convinced that he would soon be taking his last breath. Once again, Johannes cried out to God—this time, in complete darkness.

Suddenly, Johannes felt a comforting hand embrace his arm and touch his hand. He could see no one, but the touch was peaceful, reassuring. He shouted, "Who is it, and how did you get here in the middle of the jungle when no one has been in sight?" The jungle was silent.

The person with the comforting touch had suddenly disappeared, but miraculously, Johannes felt a warm surge of energy. He regained enough strength to continue on.

Later, Johannes's brother-in-law discovered him injured in the jungle. Johannes said he believed the comforting visitor was Jesus because he had found no one, only countless corpses, during his eight-day quest for help in the jungle.

Today, twenty-year-old Johannes sees his multiple scars as badges of honor for Jesus. He says he forgives his attackers as "our Father in heaven forgives us." He takes Jesus' command in

Matthew 6:15 seriously: "But if you do not forgive men their sins, your Father will not forgive your sins."

Johannes is studying to become an evangelist. He says God spared his life so that he may lead many Muslims to Christ.

Johannes could depend only on the Lord. He had no other option. But that's only because he had lived each day in total dependence—it was his habit, his lifestyle. Today, he continues to depend on God.

Learning to Doubt Our Doubts

As we saw in the last chapter, those who model heroic faith are motivated by what others aren't aware of—they draw upon an invisible reality; they see life from God's point of view. But even the most focused can have doubts, especially during lonely nights of hardship and suffering. Separated from family and friends and surrounded by enemies, we can wonder, "Where is God?" or "What is God doing?" or even "Why me?" That's what makes Christian martyrs so remarkable—even during their darkest days, they steadfastly cling to their faith, depending completely on their Lord.

"You may destroy my body, but not my soul," the brave Korean pastor responded to the invading Communist army of North Korea, and he continued to boldly declare his faith in Christ.

As Pastor Im spoke, the officer's anger intensified, until he said with disgust, "If you do not care for yourself, then think of your family. They will be killed also."

Pastor Im hesitated. He expected to be hurt but had not considered what might happen to his family. Yet, knowing the choice he had to make, he calmly replied to the Communist officer, "I would rather have my wife and babies die by your gun, knowing that they and I stood faithful, than to betray my Lord and save them."

Pastor Im was led away to a dark prison cell. For two years, he kept up his courage by reciting a Bible verse that was precious to him. Every day from his small isolated cell, others could hear Pastor Im recite in a loving, calm voice John 13:7, where Jesus promised, "You do not realize now what I am doing, but later you will understand."

This courageous man could defeat doubts and depend wholly on God because he knew his Savior and remembered his promise.

Dr. V. Raymond Edman, a former president of Wheaton College, used to encourage students, "Never doubt in darkness what God has shown you in the light." We may not find ourselves attacked like Johannes Mantahari or imprisoned like Pastor Im, but other forms of darkness can dim our vision of God, causing us to wonder if he really loves us, or even cares. That's where we must rehearse his promises and remember his powerful work on our behalf . . . "in the light." This will happen naturally if we have learned to "practice his presence."

"Never doubt in darkness what God has shown you in the light."

Learning to Practice God's Presence

Brother Lawrence, a seventeenth-century monk, has been credited with coining the expression "practicing the presence of God." It's the title of his classic book on prayer. When Nicholas Herman was born in 1605, he had no idea how his life would play out. Only after years of military service in Europe did he surrender to an ordered life of devotion and prayer with the Carmelite monks and assume the name history has associated with him.

For Brother Lawrence, prayer was more than formal phrases spoken at defined times of the day while kneeling before a cross in the chapel. It included kneeling on a dirty kitchen floor in the monastery. There he would talk to God, as to a friend, as he went about his daily task of washing the floor or peeling potatoes. While weeding the garden, he would converse with his heavenly Father about unwanted growths within his life that needed to be pulled.

In *Practicing the Presence of God*, Brother Lawrence writes, "There is not in the world a kind of life more sweet and delightful, than that of a continual conversation with God: those only can comprehend it who practice and experience it. . . . It is a great delusion to think our times of prayer ought to differ from other times. We are as strictly obliged to cleave to God by action in the time of action as by prayer in the season of prayer."

His point is that when we keep the communication lines open with God, conversing with him continually (not just during times of crisis), listening for his voice, and looking for his work, then we will be prepared for those difficult times that will surely come. If we depend on God during our daily, mundane routines, we will depend on him under pressure and in the dark.

Not all who have demonstrated heroic faith have been privileged to read Brother Lawrence's book. Nonetheless, they have discovered his secret. By maintaining a conscious dependence on the Lord, they prove that the apostle Paul's injunction to "pray continually" (1 Thessalonians 5:17) really is possible.

When a person consciously visualizes the Lord's presence at all times, he or she gains confidence to face whatever a day may bring. Or as one person has delightfully observed, "There is nothing that the Lord and I can't handle together!" Like those times when a month's pay disappears before the month does. When conflicts on the job undermine one's sense of accomplishment or mission. When heartaches with teenage children drive you to distraction and to your knees. When coworkers ridicule you for doing what is right.

Do any of these examples sound familiar? What can you do to practice God's presence?

Margaret Powers understood the fact that close proximity to the Lord does not insulate a person from disaster or suffering. Still, she was forced to embrace the reality that when we depend on the Lord at such times we are not disappointed. Mrs. Powers is the artistic wordsmith who wrote that powerful poem "Footprints in the Sand." In it, she describes a dream a man had about walking side by side with the Lord along a beach. Juxtaposed footprints documented that reassuring reality. Looking at those footprints during the most difficult time in his life, however, the man saw only a single set of steps. But, as the poem points out, even though the man wondered if the Lord had deserted him at that time, nothing could have been further from the truth. Rather, the Lord had been carrying him.

Margaret Powers not only wrote those inspiring words in the mid-1960s, she has lived them. When she and her husband were in the process of moving from their home in British Columbia, this poem and hundreds of others were stolen. For more than two decades "Footprints in the Sand" was published on posters, greeting cards, and bookmarks, attributed to "Anonymous." Tens of thousands of dollars in royalties that rightly belonged to the author of the poem were never paid, while card companies and publishers were making a small fortune on her work.

For many years Margaret tried in vain to prove her ownership of the poem. She knew that God had given her those words to encourage his people. But now she felt abandoned by him. Where was he when she needed him? Where was the vindication to which she felt entitled? All she could do was appeal her cause to him in prayer and rest in his arms. In the process, she found that though the cost may be high, fully depending on the Lord in the midst of unfair circumstances is worth it. When Margaret was eventually recognized as the poem's source, the compensation she received was insignificant compared to the security she had discovered in her Father's arms.

A Page from King David's Diary

Many times in King David's life, as he walked along the sands of the Judean wilderness, he could see only one set of footprints. David knew what it felt like to despair of life itself. He wrote Psalm 22 on such an occasion. This brutally candid page out of David's journal begins, "My God, my God, why have you forsaken me?"

Running for his life, David felt like an uncaged canary in the presence of the cat king about to pounce on him. As he dodged Saul at every turn, David wondered why God was noticeably absent. He had known the Lord's companionship throughout his life but not at that time. He felt helpless, hopeless, and abandoned. "Why are you so far from saving me, so far from the words of my groaning?" he declared.

Who hasn't felt like David? "What's the use of praying?" he likely wondered. "I feel so alone. I have no indication that anyone is listening; yet, unless God intervenes, there is nothing anyone can do." When did you feel that way? Johannes Mantahari knows what that's like. So does Margaret Powers. "O my God, I cry out by day, but you do not answer" (v. 2).

What is remarkable about this psalm, however, is that David continued to express his dependence on God even though he didn't think the Lord was anywhere to be found. David felt abandoned, but he proceeded to bend his knee and pray. His words of candid complaint were not blasphemous explosions of anger. Although they betrayed the despair of his heart, they were darts of prayer aimed in the Lord's direction.

As we read through the rest of Psalm 22, we can detect a shift in David's perspective. About midway through his journal entry, he recognized that he had reason to believe God was in control and could be trusted to deliver him. For David, the single set of footprints in the sand suggested the same conclusion that Margaret Powers came to.

Curiously, when we are going through "dark valleys" and need to be reminded of the immediacy of the Lord's presence, we often turn to Psalm 23. But the psalm that immediately precedes it contains just as much encouragement and perhaps even more honesty to which we can personally relate. Psalm 22 is a harbinger of hope to the fainthearted. In addition to giving us a glimpse into the heart of a man who is very much like us, it gives us permission to talk to God at all times (and especially when we aren't feeling very godly or when we feel as though he doesn't care).

The beauty of practicing the presence of God is the uncomplicated definition of prayer it promotes. If we talk to God while commuting to work or biking to school or preparing supper in the kitchen, we do not have to be concerned with saying the right words in the right place. It's a lifestyle more than a learned procedure. And if, in that ongoing communion of words or thoughts directed to the Lord, we know we can be transparently open with God about what we are feeling, we can come right out and ask him if we should believe (or disbelieve) thoughts that enter our heads.

The beauty of practicing the presence of God is the uncomplicated definition of prayer it promotes.

Similar in tone to "Footprints" is a lesser-known verse by Reg Simak. This poem invites the reader to be confident of God's everlasting arms when capsized by hardships or sinking in a sea of despair. It is a call to acknowledge our dependency on him.

Wash over me, dear Father, with the power of the sea
Flood me with a sense of peace that can only come from Thee.

As the undertow of panic seeks to suck me to the ground,
would you cause your mighty waves to beach me where it's safe and sound?
And then as you have done before please do it once again.
Won't you carry me within your arms as we walk along the sand?

A Countercultural Concept

While demonstrating one's dependence on God through prayer is a mark of heroic faith, the posture it requires is not esteemed by our culture. Acknowledging dependence on someone or something is viewed as a weakness. Admitting a lack of strength or confessing a physical or emotional limitation is frowned upon. People spend millions of dollars a year on cosmetics to coverup imperfections. They spend as much if not more on designer clothes, hoping that an insignia or logo on a sweater or shirt will cause people they want to impress to look at the label instead of at their eyes, which betray the lack of purpose in their lives.

The United States of America was born out of a revolution spawned by a political dependence on England. America's military victory was sealed by a carefully written document that declared her independence. Not only did it set the political tone for the new nation, the Declaration of Independence ushered in a cultural climate that breeds self-made individuals and celebrates unilateral achievement. Within such an atmosphere of independence, a reluctance to admit one's need of others or needs of any kind developed.

King David's son, Solomon, did not embrace all that his father tried to teach him. This son of a woman whom David married after an illicit affair with her would prove to have an inexhaustible sexual appetite. His wives and concubines numbered in the hundreds. His confessions in Ecclesiastes offer a window to his permissive past. Still Solomon, the wise and wealthy king, did learn from his father the importance of acknowledging his need of God.

In Proverbs 3:5–6, Solomon not only documents the value of ongoing communication that he witnessed between David and the Lord, he also celebrates the wisdom of acknowledging one's dependence on God. He writes "Trust in the LORD with all your heart and lean not on your own understanding; in all your ways acknowledge him, and he will make your paths straight."

If only Solomon had heeded his own advice, his list of regrets at the end of his life would have been markedly reduced. But, sadly, the king who received the wisdom he requested of the Lord, failed to incorporate the power of the Proverbs into his daily pursuits. Because of that, we would not be inclined to include Solomon as one who modeled heroic faith. Those who qualify for that title incorporate what they know to be true into what they do day in and day out. People like Todd Beamer.

Heroic Faith on Flight 93

Prior to September 11, the name Todd Beamer was not widely known. Since that infamous date his name has become synonymous with heroism and faith. In the final moments of his life, this thirty-two-year-old American businessman acknowledged his dependence on God by calling out to him in prayer, a practice that for Todd Beamer was as natural as drawing a breath.

Following the customary safety demonstration and one final seat check, United Flight 93 taxied down the Newark runway and took off. As Flight 93 approached Cleveland airspace, the Boeing 757 turned sharply to the left and began flying south. Within a few minutes, Todd and others realized that something had gone terribly wrong. Four terrorists had commandeered the plane, killing the pilot and copilot. As best as can be pieced together, the terrorists at the controls of United Flight 93 were planning to crash into the White House or another target. With both towers of the World Trade Center in New York and the Pentagon having been attacked already, authorities were on full alert when it became known that the flight over Pennsylvania had veered dramatically from its flight plan.

Fearing the worst, several passengers used personal cell phones to call loved ones to say good-bye. Todd used the phone above his tray table. Because he wasn't able to get through to Lisa, his pregnant wife, he was connected with an operator at GTE Airfone headquarters. When he described the chilling details of what was taking place on the plane, the operator transferred Todd to a GTE supervisor.

Todd proceeded to give the woman on the other end of the phone a message to deliver to his wife if he did not survive the flight. The woman promised to personally convey it to Lisa. Then, amazingly calm though he knew death was imminent, Todd asked the supervisor to pray the Lord's Prayer with him. She agreed. It was Todd's way of committing his life, his family, and the surreal circumstances in which he found himself to his heavenly Father.

It was one final reminder that his call as a follower of Jesus was to forgive those who trespass against him. At the conclusion of praying, "for Thine is the kingdom and the power and the glory forever. Amen," just before the line went dead, the supervisor heard Todd spontaneously add, "Help me, Jesus!" Then he turned to his fellow passengers with whom he had hatched a plan to overtake the terrorists and said those five words that have become Todd Beamer's epitaph: "Are you ready? Let's roll!"

As a result of the resistance that Todd Beamer and the others offered, the plot to take out another symbol of American freedom was foiled. United Flight 93 crashed in rural Pennsylvania, killing all aboard but no one on the ground.

Todd's strong commitment to Jesus never wavered. When death pulled up the blinds and stared him in the face, this young believer did not flinch. The reason was quite clear. He lived each day with a sense of dependence on God. He began each day in prayer, and he prayed with his two young sons. Being raised in a home where prayer was taught and practiced, Todd caught his parents' passion for communicating with the Lord. When Todd was just a toddler, his mom taught him the prayer that he prayed on Flight 93.

Early in life, Todd made his parents' faith his own. As a young husband and father, he continued to live out his faith in practical ways. At the time of his death, Todd and his wife, Lisa, were involved in a home Bible study group. And guess what the group was studying? They were scouring the various Gospel accounts of the Lord's Prayer in an attempt to make personal application to their lives. As it turns out, Todd ended his earthly life the way he lived it every day. He surrendered it in prayer.

Todd Beamer was not killed because he believed in Christ. And he wouldn't qualify as a representative of the "persecuted church." Yet he stands as a powerful example of living in dependence on God. Whether or not we ever experience pain and suffering for our faith, God wants us to depend on him—in our decisions, on the job, with our families and futures. A quick check of our wallets would reveal the American slogan, "In God we trust." That's a nice sentiment, but do we? Or does our trust rest in the coins and bills that bear the phrase?

Me Ling was young when she was arrested for her Christian activities in Communist China. During their interrogations, the police would torture Me Ling to try to force her to betray friends in the underground church.

"I also found that when I purified my heart of the fear of men, I learned to really see God."

At first Me Ling was extremely fearful, and she wondered what purpose God could have for her in that terrible place. But then she remembered the teachings of her pastor, who had said, "Real suffering lasts only a minute, and then we spend eternity with our awesome Savior." She knew she could depend on God, in life or in death.

When asked how she was able to keep from going crazy during her imprisonment and torture, Me Ling replied, "When I closed my eyes, I could not see the angry faces of the men or the instruments of pain they were using. I kept repeating the promise of Christ to myself: 'Blessed are the pure in heart, for they will see God' (Matthew 5:8). I also found that when I purified my heart of the fear of men, I learned to really see God. I took courage from all the others who had gone before me and focused on him until everything else faded away. When the officials learned of my defense, they taped my eyelids open. But it was too late because my vision was secure."

Me Ling was independent of this world because she had declared her dependence on God.

Inking Your Own Declaration of Dependence

■ Passionately admitting our helplessness is a key to experiencing the joy of God's presence. Rather than praying as you normally do, experiment by calling out to the Lord with humility and candor.

■ Think of a time in your life when you felt "forsaken by God" but later realized that he had carried you. Write out that experience. Keep it handy as a testimony the Lord may desire you to share with someone who claims that God has abandoned him or her.

■ Honestly answer this question: Where is my security—in what am I placing my trust? Then talk to God about your answer and ask him for the strength to depend totally on him.

■ Contemplate the patterns of persistent prayer that marked the lives of Johannes Mantahari and Todd Beamer. What could you do at work, at school, at home, in the car, and elsewhere to "practice the presence of God"?

■ Me Ling learned how to "see God," even during intense suffering. Take a few minutes: Close your eyes and visualize your "persecutors," those associates, neighbors, and others who don't appreciate your faith or Christian stand. As each face comes to mind, try to see God's image in them and ask God to help you love them for his sake.

CHAPTER 3

Love of God's Word

Bookworms of Truth

It's bound to make a difference.
The Word of God has been preserved
in order to preserve those
who bow to its authority.
Heroes are nourished
by the pages of living truth.
Like bookworms,
they devour and digest
what others disregard.
And though it's sometimes hard,
they contemplate and then relate
what God says to their lives.

BY GREG ASIMAKOUPOULOS

AS WE HAVE SEEN, those who distinguish themselves by lives of extreme faith are mindful of the transitory nature of this life. They have learned to live in a state of constant dependence on the Lord. They also can be identified by their reverence toward God's Word and their devoted attempts to be channels of its truth.

Six weeks after the terrorist attacks in America, Muslim terrorists interrupted a church service in Bahawalpur, Pakistan. Three gunmen entered through the back of the building. One of them charged up to the pulpit and ordered the pastor to throw his Bible to the ground. Emmanuel alAtta clutched his Bible to his heart, turned his back on the terrorist, and said, "I will not." To the horror of the congregation, the terrorist shot him in the back as Pastor Emmanuel's wife and children looked on. The Pakistani minister was not the only victim that day. The terrorists in the attack killed several others.

Some might wonder why Pastor Emmanuel didn't comply with the terrorist's demand to drop his Bible. Throwing a Bible to the ground might have been viewed as a personal violation of honor, but it would not have been a sin. But Pastor Emmanuel knew what such an act would symbolize to a radical Muslim attacker. Muslims consider any disrespect to the Koran to be blasphemous. So they would probably view throwing a Bible on the floor to be a rejection of Christianity. In their minds, such an act would convey that the Bible is not really the holy truth of God Christians proclaim it to be.

No doubt Pastor Emmanuel could have complied with the order and thrown down the Bible, knowing he could explain to everyone later that Christians don't have the same ideas about the Bible as Muslims do about the Koran. But who's to say the terrorists wouldn't have made further demands of him and then shot him anyway? Even if they wouldn't have shot him, those who knew Pastor Emmanuel believe he would not have dropped the Bible. He refused to obey the command because he could not imagine his last act on earth being a disgrace to what was so precious to him. He loved God's Word enough to make eternally sure no one would ever misunderstand his commitment to it.

What do you think you would have done in a similar situation? Are you *that* devoted to the Bible?

A Prized Possession

Such a devotion to the Scriptures is rare in the United States, where the average home has multiple copies on coffee tables, bookshelves, and nightstands. Western believers enjoy Bibles in scores of varieties, in several translations and in every size, color, and binding. We have Bibles for children, kids, teens, mothers, and fathers, "study Bibles," "devotional Bibles," and many other selections. Older Christians can boast of owning a dozen or more copies. Perhaps that's why we find it easy to take the Bible for granted. In a country like Pakistan, however, where Bibles are scarce, Christians cherish the Scriptures as a priceless possession. In countries where owning it is outlawed, the Bible's sacredness is heightened for those who risk arrest or injury in order to protect a copy—every copy is treasured.

A Korean believer shared this: "They begged and begged me, but I couldn't give it to them. I know Christians are supposed to share, but I just couldn't part with it." Then he held out his hand, revealing his prized possession.

"I really wanted to, but I couldn't," the man continued. "You see, people in North Korea told me that they have been praying for fifty years to get a Bible. But I didn't give them mine because I had been praying for twenty years, and I had just gotten it from a pastor in South Korea." The man hugged his Bible to his chest. He had just escaped the Communist prison state and was now living freely in South Korea.

Despite the fact that fervent respect for God's Word is not as discernible among Christians in North America as it is in Muslim countries or Eastern bloc nations, don't be misled. Many in the West take the Bible seriously and, as a result, are ostracized in cities or towns where steeples and crosses dot the skyline. Or to put it more succinctly, Christians are persecuted in places where the prominent religious faith is Christianity. Candidates for

Candidates for heroic faith don't always have dramatic life-and-death testimonies. Often, they are people like you.

heroic faith don't always have dramatic life-and-death testimonies. Often, they are people like you.

But stop for a moment and consider: Would you be on that list? Do you take the Bible seriously?

A Legacy of Love

It's no coincidence that an identifiable marker in all of these believers' lives is a love of God's Word. Those who are aware of heaven's grandstands pictured in Hebrews 12:1 have a sense of what is necessary to be seated with the heroes who have completed their race. But a high regard for the Word is not a recent phenomenon. It has been an indicator of heroic faith a long time. Believers have bled and died for the Scriptures for centuries. Consider Timothy and Maura.

"Tell him, Timothy, please!" Maura pleaded with her husband. "Tell the governor where the Scriptures are hidden and be free! I cannot bear to watch any more of this." Timothy and Maura, residents of the Roman province of Mauritania, had been married only a few short weeks before their arrest.

Timothy had refused the governor's demand, and Maura had watched in horror as Roman soldiers burned out his eyes with hot irons. Now Timothy was hanging upside down, with a weight hanging around his neck. As Timothy waited for his gag to be removed, the fear that he had felt at his arrest was replaced with a divine calm.

But then, instead of renouncing his faith and disclosing the location of his church's copies of the Scriptures as the soldiers expected, Timothy scolded his young wife. "Do not let your love for me come before your love for Christ," he urged her. Seeing her husband's courage, Maura's own resolve was strengthened. Enraged by Timothy's refusal and Maura's newfound courage, Governor Arrianus sentenced them to the harshest tortures of the Roman world. Yet, they refused to break and deny Christ. Eventually, they were crucified, side by side.

Centuries later, in 1519, six men and a widow stood in court, convicted of committing an extreme crime against the church. Their crime? Teaching their children the Lord's Prayer and the Ten Commandments in the English language. At that time Latin was the only language allowed for biblical instruction in England; yet, the common people spoke English. Believers had secretly translated parts of the Bible into English, however, and had carefully passed the translations from home to home. But these believers had been caught and convicted and sentenced to be burned at the stake.

At the end of the proceedings, the widow was pardoned, allowed to go free. No one protested because she was alone and had young children at home. As her guard walked her to her house, he heard a rustling within the woman's coat sleeve. He pulled from her coat the English translations, the same materials that the convicted believers had been teaching their children. Even though this woman had just escaped a death sentence, she refused to part with the translations, believing that her children still needed to know the truth of God's Word. This sealed her fate. Soon after, the six men and one woman were secured to wooden poles and burned alive.

A few years later, also in England, William Tyndale was engaged in a heated discussion with a learned theologian.

"Master Tyndale, you must admit," scoffed the learned doctor of theology, "that men are better with the laws of the church that they can understand than God's own law in the Bible!"

Tyndale responded strongly: "I defy the priests and their laws! If God sees fit to let me live, then it won't be long before any boy who drives a plough will know the Scriptures better than they do!" This remark divided Tyndale and the established church. He soon fled England for the mainland, where he produced his outlaw version of the New Testament in English. Then, for years, these small New Testaments were smuggled in bales of cotton, aboard German ships, and in any other place where they could secretly enter England. Eventually, however, Tyndale was betrayed by a "friend" and tried for heresy.

During his year in prison awaiting execution, Tyndale finished much of the Old Testament translation in English. His last words before being burned at the stake in October of 1536 were, "Lord! Open the king's eyes!"

God did. Only a year after Tyndale's martyrdom, the monarchy allowed the first English Bible to be legally printed. The King James Authorized Version appeared seventy-four years later. Today's King James Version of the Bible matches an estimated 83 percent of Tyndale's work word for word.

Hungering for God's Word

In his book *What in the World Is God Doing?* (Waco, TX: Word Publishing, 1978), Dr. Ted Engstrom, former president of World Vision, relates a story told by a Korean believer. The story concerns three Korean workmen who found jobs in China in the 1880s. While in China they heard the gospel and embraced the Lord Jesus as Savior. The three soon were determined to find a way to get the message of Christ into their own country. They knew it would not be easy, however, because the Korean government forbade evangelizing.

Since the Korean and Chinese alphabets were similar, they decided to try to smuggle a copy of the Chinese Bible into their homeland. They drew straws to see who would have the privilege of bringing the gospel into Korea. The first man buried the Bible in his belongings and headed toward the border, a journey of many days by footpath. There he was searched, found out, and executed. Word reached the others that their friend had been killed. The second man tore pages from his Bible and hid the separate pages throughout his luggage. He, too, made the long trip to the border only to be searched and beheaded.

Filled with a relentless passion to do what his colleagues had not been able to do and determined to succeed, the third man ingeniously tore his Bible apart page by page. Next, he folded each page into tiny strips and wove the strips into a rope. He then proceeded to wrap his baggage with the homemade rope. When he came to the border, the guards asked him to unwrap his belongings. Finding nothing amiss, they admitted him.

The man arrived home, untied the rope, and ironed out each page. He reassembled his Bible and began to preach Christ wherever he went. And when the missionaries of the late nineteenth century fanned into Korea, they found the seed already sown and the first fruits appearing.

We share a legacy of devotion, of passion really, for God's Word—reading it, studying it, obeying it, and sharing it with oth-

In the first century, devotion to God's Word was synonymous with the word disciple.

ers. In every generation since the time that Jesus challenged Satan with the innate human hunger for God's truth ("Man does not live on bread alone, but on every word that comes from the mouth of God"—Matthew 4:4), an appetite for the Scriptures has marked devoted believers. In fact, in the first century, devotion to God's Word was synonymous with the word *disciple.*

A First-Century Thirst

A Jewish physician by the name of Luke took it upon himself to compile a cogent compendium of the life of Jesus and the history of the early Christian Church. His motivation was an anonymous Roman official who most likely had been a recent, secret convert to Christianity. Even though Luke addressed both the Gospel that bears his name and his sequel (the Acts of the Apostles) to a man by the name of Theophilus, this probably was not the man's name. In Greek, *Theophilus* means "lover of God," thus, it was in all probability a coded name for someone who was not prepared to publicly confess his faith.

Because Dr. Luke had been a companion of the apostle Paul, he had access to reliable eyewitness accounts. He wrote to "Theophilus" to encourage this dear brother by reporting the signs and wonders that marked the ministry of Jesus and the evidence of God's faithfulness that marked the ministry of the emerging church. In the second chapter of Acts, Dr. Luke describes the priorities and activities of that first congregation in Jerusalem:

They devoted themselves to the apostles' teaching and to the fellowship, to the breaking of bread and to prayer. Everyone was filled with awe, and many wonders and miraculous signs were done by the apostles. All the believers were together and had everything in common. Selling their possessions and goods, they gave to anyone as he had need. Every day they continued to meet together in the temple courts. They broke bread in their homes and ate together with glad and sincere hearts, praising God and enjoying the favor of all the people. And the Lord added to their number daily those who were being saved. (Acts 2:42–47)

The word that jumps from the page is *devoted.* This is the Greek word *proskartereo,* which means "to be earnest towards something," "to persevere," "to be constantly diligent," or "to adhere closely to." To say a person is devoted means more than a casual observance or a religious practice. It suggests an intense commitment. That's the word Luke carefully chose, under the inspiration of the Holy Spirit, to describe this first generation of Jesus people. They were devoted to being with one another. They were devoted to the Lord by honoring his Supper. They were devoted to a lifestyle of prayer (both formal prayer services in the temple courts as well as informal times of prayer in one another's homes).

Luke first calls attention to the fact that they devoted themselves to "the apostles' teaching." Obviously, this refers to the preaching and teaching of the original followers of Jesus. It certainly included the truth of God they had derived from their three years of traveling with Jesus and listening to his words. The four Gospels of the

New Testament are proof of that. It is also safe to assume that the apostles' teaching included commentary on the Old Testament that the Lord had taught them. In other words, the early church devoted themselves to the Scriptures. It was their daily bread.

Ironically, when Luke wrote this description of the Jerusalem church, Christianity was a threat to the Roman Empire. Christians were being hunted, imprisoned, and killed. His words recall a peaceful time when non-Christians who observed Christ's followers were favorably impressed with what they witnessed. In all likelihood, the reason Luke could easily describe the priorities of the pre-persecuted congregation is because those now tortured for their faith continued to be devoted to the Word of God, fellowship, the Lord's Supper, and prayer.

Taking a Breath in Suffocating Times

Trials and hardships don't undermine one's devotion to the truth of Scripture. As with the wilderness Jesus faced, when we are deprived of what we find comforting or comfortable, we recognize our need for nourishment that can come only from the Word of God. When we are thirsting for God's touch in our lives, the Bible is an oasis that floods us with a sense of his power. It is like the refreshment and awe we experience when we stand beneath a cascading waterfall. In other words, those whose lives are marked by a love for God's Word have most likely been marked by heartache. During times of struggle, they discover how refreshing and indispensable it is. The Bible becomes the very air they breathe. As a result, when the wilderness gives way to flowering meadows or lovely alpine vistas, they remain devoted to the Scriptures.

Following the unexpected and tragic death of a work colleague, Marie Barnett expressed her grief by casting herself on the Lord. Words began filling her broken heart, and before she knew it, she was pouring them out to her heavenly Father in a spontaneous song of devotion. The lyrics celebrated her love of the Lord and his Word. As far as Marie was concerned, that was all she had to hold on to. His presence through the Holy Spirit and the Scriptures was like oxygen to her suffocating soul.

In the years that have passed since Marie first sang "Breathe" in 1995, Christians around the world have echoed her love of God's presence and Word. Each week, millions still lift their voices with this song, prayerfully identifying his holy presence with the very air that they breathe and God's Word with their daily bread. And the song's familiar refrain affirms desperation for God and the truth that we are utterly lost without him.

A Hero Named Hal

The church Hal Barnes attends doesn't sing Marie Barnett's chorus, but Hal attests to the truth of her lyrics. Hal Barnes has not been "persecuted" in the sense that we ordinarily think of the word, but he has known the sting of put-downs. On more occasions than he can recall, those who don't understand his fascination with the Savior or his love of God's Word have misunderstood him.

Hal was born in 1917. He was musically inclined and intelligent enough to get into Stanford. But for years he struggled to be accepted in the eyes of his older brother, an internationally known intellect—a scholar and inventor.

Life did not come as easy for Hal. Because he did not have the IQ of his brother, he found a career in sales. Hal did well but was not content. His church attendance didn't equate to a personal relationship with Jesus. Among the files in his three-drawer cabinet, church was just another file that he would pull out once a week.

But at the age of forty, Hal's life changed dramatically. While watching a Billy Graham crusade on television with his wife, Juanita, he recognized his need of a personal savior. They started attending Des Plaines Bible Church in suburban Chicago. And Hal started memorizing God's Word.

His daughter Chandler recalls, "During his business trips, Daddy used the time in his car, in between calling on clients, to commit large chunks of Scripture to memory. He kept a small paperbound copy of the Bible that would fit in his shirt pocket."

With God's truth in easy access, Hal took the injunctions of the psalmist seriously. He literally hid the Word in his heart. Although business colleagues thought his practices a bit odd and began calling him "Hallelujah Hal," he took their swipes in stride. Hal was no longer vulnerable to what others thought. In the Word of God he had finally found assurance of God's unconditional love and acceptance. Freed from his previous prison of an inferiority complex, Hal was confident in his standing before the Lord.

As this amazing man approached his eighty-fifth birthday, that confidence was tested by the most difficult ordeal he ever faced. Juanita, his wife of fifty-nine years, died the week after September 11, 2001. While New Yorkers grieved the loss of three thousand victims to the terrorists' attacks, Hal dealt with the death of his best friend. But in his dog-eared Bible, he found the resources he needed to face the rest of his life alone.

To date, Hal Barnes has memorized 173 chapters of the Bible. More impressive, however, is the degree to which he has allowed the truth of those passages to be filtered through his life. Not long ago he stood before a roomful of family and friends at his grandson's thirteenth birthday party. Holding up his leather-bound copy of the Scriptures, Hal challenged the boy to become a lover of God's Word. "Take it from me, grandson of mine. Let the Bible transform your life. Hide it in your heart. This book will keep you from sin, or sin will keep you from this book."

The Transforming Power of God's Word

If this young man heeds his grandfather's wise advice, he will be well on his way to creating a legacy of heroic faith that he will one day be able to leave to *his* grandchildren.

What legacy of faith will you leave? Do your loved ones, friends, and coworkers know how the Bible impacts your life?

Youth are particularly impressionable. That is when the seeds of a distinctive faith are sown. Gary Lane, a worker with The Voice of the Martyrs (VOM), has seen that firsthand.

During a visit two years ago to Chiang Mai, Thailand, Gary met more than a dozen young Shan boys who had served as child soldiers in an anti-Burmese government militia. In the sovereign plan of God, Shan leaders allowed missionaries to take the boys to live in a Christian orphanage near Chiang Mai.

As Gary Lane recounted, "Just three weeks after their arrival

"You mean, this is God's Word . . . the word of God on paper, on the pages of a book?" said one seventeen-year-old boy.

in Thailand, the boys accepted Christ and converted from Buddhism and animism to Christianity. The boys were in awe when first introduced to the Bible.

"You mean, this is God's Word . . . the word of God on paper, on the pages of a book?" said one seventeen-year-old boy. His almond-shaped eyes opened wide as he stared in wonder at the Bible he had just been given. The boy clutched the Bible to his chest, cherishing the gift as if he had been given a valuable gem or a brick of gold.

The workers at the orphanage say they have witnessed a miracle—they've seen many changes in the Shan boys since they came to Christ. These loud, aggressive, indifferent, and often violent former boy-soldiers are now humble, meek, loving, and caring young men. Because they view God's Word with reverence and awe, and because they are true lovers of God's Word, they read it regularly, strive to follow it, and walk in obedience to the Lord—they are complete in him. The transformation they have made is the evidence—it is how we know they are in him. The Shan former boy-soldiers who were trained to fight and kill are now walking as Jesus did.

Before VOM founder Richard Wurmbrand died in 2001, he had celebrated many milestones in his lifelong journey to serve the persecuted church. When China was opened to outsiders forty years after the iron curtain closed, he rejoiced with the exponential growth of the church in the midst of suffering and persecution. When Communism collapsed in the Soviet Union, he praised God for answered prayer. Still, countless Chinese and Russian Christians continue to suffer. Many of them have languished, and still languish, in prison. Many have been martyred. What Pastor Wurmbrand wrote in his book *Alone with God* (Bartlesville, OK: Living Sacrifice Book Company, 1999) some years back, remains a sobering reminder of our call to pray for our sisters and brothers who are tortured for their faith and to be inspired by their reverence for God's Word:

> In Chungking, at one time, Bibles and other Christian books were being burned in public. Christians were forced to look on. However, Bibles are thick books and burn slowly. Oxygen has difficulty in getting between the pages, of which there are about one thousand. An onlooker took advantage of this fact to tear out for himself a page from one of the burning Bibles. For years afterwards, the underground congregation to which he belonged nourished its faith from this one page. Then they succeeded in smuggling out a short report of what had happened. "We have learned from this one page that trying to be a better Christian is wrong. Christ does not want better Christians but Christians who resemble Christ," they added.
>
> Upon hearing about this, we tried to find out which page of the Bible they had in their possession. It was the page which contains Matthew 16:18 with the verse, "Thou art Peter, and upon this rock I will build my church; and the gates of hell shall not prevail against it." From such a promise one can live. (p. 121)

What Made the Difference?

Why did Pastor Emmanuel, Timothy, Maura, the courageous widow, William Tyndale, the Korean workers, and countless others give their lives to protect, translate, and share God's Word? That's the key question because it has profound implications for how we live out our faith.

The answer: These men and women didn't love the Bible because they believed it; they loved the Bible because they knew it was truly God's Word and because they *lived* it. The Bible, or the part they had, was more than a collection of words on paper; it was the truth of God. Their resulting actions, therefore, were not based on passion but on obedience. Walking in obedience to God is an adventure, no matter where we live. But that adventure will be misguided unless we allow God's Word to be absorbed into every part of our lives.

As VOM works in difficult areas of the world, one Scripture passage is often the topic of sermons or thoughts—Romans 8:39, which states that nothing can separate believers from God's love.

In Sudan, Pastor Abram witnessed the suffering of his people. Bibles are rare in his country; in fact, his congregation of four hundred has only one Bible. He has seen people give their lives for the little Scripture they have. Sudanese believers have been tortured, starved, and even killed for refusing to accept Islam.

When VOM visited Sudan and delivered hundreds of Bibles to Pastor Abram for his congregation, he gave the VOM workers his battered and worn Bible. The pages barely held together, and one page was especially worn—Romans 8. Think of how many times Pastor Abram must have reflected on this passage for his own strength and how many times he must have used it to encourage members of his congregation as they stood together against war and persecution. Perhaps he passed that single page from house to house.

The truth of the matter is simply this: The ultimate message of the Bible is the story of God's love for humankind and the fact that he sent his own Son to die for our sins. *Nothing* can separate us from God's love.

Heroes of faith have this source for their strength—God's love in their hearts. They know they can never be separated from God's love, and they never separate his love and his truth from the written Word.

Days after the VOM team met with Pastor Abram, he was gunned down by radical Islamic soldiers from northern Sudan.

If we're not living out our faith in Christ, we will find it difficult to experience the power of God's Word that is a regular part of life for many persecuted believers. For them, the words of Dr. Luke are still being written.

Do you love God's Word? Is Bible study a regular part of your weekly routine? When you understand Scripture and what God wants, do you obey him? Bible reading, studying, applying, meditating, and memorizing should be as important to us as breathing.

Learning How to Breathe

- If your hunger and thirst for Scripture has waned in recent days, chances are you have enjoyed a season of prosperity and blessing that has resulted in the beginnings of a plateauing faith. One way to work up an appetite for God's Word is to take an honest look at where you are with the Lord. So where are you?

Check your schedule and carve out a good half-hour to come before him. Begin your time with God by thanking him for everything good in your life right now. Next, ask God to bring to mind those values and behaviors that have started to slide as a result of the way you have managed his blessings. Listen for what he will say.

▣ Where is your Bible? What steps do you need to take to begin a program of regular Bible study?

▣ Nothing primes the pump of a well like a little water. Go ahead and dip into the Bible for verses you have previously underlined or highlighted. Read them and rediscover the truth of a particular passage that caused you to underline that verse in the first place. With each verse, ask, "Now what?" In other words, write specific ways that you can put that verse into practice in your life.

▣ Follow Hallelujah Hal's example and commit to memorize large portions of Scripture. Begin by writing down all the Bible verses you know from memory. Then add to your total by memorizing a verse a week.

▣ On another day, read Psalm 119 in one sitting. Make note of the number of times the psalmist cites "the Law of the Lord" (God's Word) as the source of wisdom, blessing, or some other attribute you desire. Then thank God for his Word and ask him to create in you a hunger for it.

Make reading, studying, and applying God's Word a regular part of your daily schedule.

CHAPTER 4

Courage

Without a Second Thought

Heroes don't faint or flinch
when the fingers of fear
attempt to pinch their arm
or punch their chin
or poke them in the eye.
They don't try to be bold,
they just are.
Heroes face disgrace
without a trace of regret.
They don't fret about what others think.
They simply do what they think they should
without a second thought.
Without fright they accept the stage
God has permitted them.
And taking their cues
from the playwright himself,
heroes act courageously.

BY GREG ASIMAKOUPOULOS

CALL IT COURAGE. For the crime of practicing his Christian faith, "Thomas" (not his real name) had been forcibly removed from his family, home, and congregation and thrown into an Eastern European prison. Once in jail this committed pastor refused to look back. Sure, he greatly missed his family. But no amount of missing would undo what had been done. Only in God's providence would he be set free. So he accepted his circumstances as within the permissible will of God and began to preach to his fellow inmates.

One Sunday as he began his message, the prison guards bolted into the room and seized Thomas. "We told you preaching was forbidden," one uniformed thug growled. "Get ready to face your punishment."

The guards hauled Thomas out of his cell and down the hall. The congregation of prisoners knew what was next. Their new friend was being taken to the "beating room."

After hearing the door slam, they heard muffled sounds, shouts, and cries. Thomas was being pummeled like a punching bag.

About an hour later the guards returned Thomas to his cell. He was bloodied and obviously bruised. His face was disfigured, yet his eyes were surprisingly bright and clear. As he looked around the large cellblock, he said, "Now, brothers, where did I leave off when we were so rudely interrupted?" Thomas proceeded to preach the rest of his message to a congregation of hungry hearts.

Yes, it's called courage. And Thomas wasn't the only imprisoned shepherd who was willing to be beaten for the privilege of providing for his incarcerated sheep. Many of these pastors are not theologically educated. Their ministerial experience is limited. Yet their determination to preach is undaunted. One such jailed preacher put it this way: "We preached and they beat. That was the deal. We were happy preaching, and they were happy beating. Everyone was happy!"

> "We preached and they beat. That was the deal. We were happy preaching, and they were happy beating. Everyone was happy!"

Acts in Action

What is acted out with regularity on the stage of contemporary history is anything but a play. The plight of the persecuted church is real-life drama that is scripted much like the pages of Scripture. Have you ever thought of the fact that Acts is the only book in the New Testament that is still being added to? When Luke wrote his second volume for that secret saint in Caesar's court, he implied something readers often miss. Unlike the Gospels, Luke didn't conclude Acts with a definitive ending. The last verse of chapter 28 pictures a persecuted Paul. Yes, he is under "house" arrest but under arrest nonetheless. We see him boldly, and without hindrance, preaching about the kingdom of God. Luke's implication is that the "acts" of the apostles would continue in observable ways. Thus, we can expect that what was true of the first disciples would be true of those who follow Jesus today.

No wonder that prison scene in some unidentified Eastern European country is like reading the pages of the New Testament. The courage that infused Pastor Thomas is a mirrored image of that which enabled Peter and John to stand up to the Jewish religious leaders in Jerusalem. In both cases, being berated or beaten did not silence those with a message to share. Similarly, in each scenario courage was not an attribute those who demonstrated it could take credit for.

A missionary with The Voice of the Martyrs (VOM) observes the following:

True courage comes through the Holy Spirit. When the Jewish Council in Acts 4 noticed that Peter and John were uneducated and untrained, the members of the Council marveled and knew the men had been with Jesus. The council members recognized Christ's power. That reminds me of today's persecuted church. These believers do not have access to seminaries and the great expanse of Christian literature and training materials that believers in the West have. They have very little knowledge, some only as much as John 3:16. They know Christ died for their sins, and that is enough knowledge to launch them into a full-time ministry of evangelizing the lost in their country. And many are willing to be persecuted and maybe even die for that "one-inch" of knowledge.

What a stark contrast from Christians in the West. Ours is a culture of Christianity where we often feel we need a depth of theological knowledge or a certain kind of life experience before we are willing to take risks in order to share our faith—risks often associated with the persecuted church; risks like being rejected by friends and family or maybe even losing a job. Actually, no additional knowledge or experience is necessary, only courage. And it is available through God's Spirit as we step out in faith. With that in mind, the percentage of faith heroes in the church entirely depends on each member's willingness to be one.

Fiction and Fact

In the 1973 edition of *Great Books of the Western World*, the compilers of the series included a special feature entitled "The Hero and the Heroic Epic." This extended article identifies three qualities that distinguished the classic "storybook hero" from human beings. First, the hero was capable of feats that ordinary men and women could not do. Second, the hero was courageous in the face of great opposition. Third, the hero experienced isolation and separation. Since no one could do what the hero was capable of doing, he or she was primarily expected to do the task alone.

Those three characteristics obviously marked such mythical

heroes as Hercules, Paul Bunyan, and Superman. But those individuals never existed.

The heroes whom we are considering in this book are not cut from make-believe cloth. They are real flesh-and-blood individuals who faced and face the same challenges we do with the same limitations.

As we have seen, some, like Thomas, are called to act out the drama of heroic faith on a stage of suffering and intense persecution. But not all. When it comes to responding to a classified ad that reads "Wanted: spiritual heroes who are known by their extreme faith," you don't have to have a prison record or have been beaten by Marxist guards or Islamic terrorists. All are eligible to apply. The heroes we have in mind are not born with special qualities. In fact, people to whom you've been introduced thus far are (from the world's point of view) about as ordinary as they come.

At times, certainly, imprisonment, kidnapping, or the need to hide has separated those with heroic faith from family, loved ones, or congregations, but isolation is not a prerequisite for exhibiting a godly lifestyle. In fact, of the three defining qualities that apply to fictional

When it comes to responding to a classified ad that reads "Wanted: spiritual heroes who are known by their extreme faith," you don't have to have a prison record or have been beaten by Marxist guards or Islamic terrorists. All are eligible to apply.

heroes, only the second one applies to spiritual heroes. To be a hero of any kind, you wear a badge of courage.

As stated earlier, however, the boldness and bravery that flow out of a believer's trust in God are not traits given to a person at birth. Courage isn't a skill that anyone feels confident putting on a résumé. It isn't a word we would use to describe ourselves. Although "courage" definitely defines those who have heroic faith, it tends to be a gift more than a given. More often than not, courage is observable only after the fact.

A Profile in Courage

Just before joining Southeast Louisiana Youth for Christ to work in their Campus Life ministry, Mike O'Hara discovered that he had a malignant tumor in his shoulder. But he felt that God had called him to youth ministry, so, after praying with his wife, he joined the staff. He immediately began to fight the cancer aggressively with radiation therapy treatments. He also started Campus Life for Abramson High School, the largest public high school in New Orleans at that time. Soon he began chemotherapy, but he continued to build the ministry.

When the cancer spread to Mike's lungs, he had several operations in Houston to remove the tumors. He scheduled those trips around club meetings and other ministry events. And every week, when he had the strength, he would go to the high school campus, walk the halls, watch athletic practices, and talk with kids. Although the chemotherapy left Mike totally bald, he didn't let his appearance deter him from his mission. Most youth workers will admit that the most difficult part of their ministry is "cold contacting"—going into the students' world to try to make friendships. Whether it's the school lunchroom or a neighbor-hood hangout, they usually feel as though they have walked into a party to which they haven't been invited. Thus, they worry about what they look like, how they will walk and stand, and what they will say. Though hairless and skinny, his body showing the effects of his painful battle against cancer, Mike would faith-fully visit the campus, walking the halls, just as he was. At times, kids who didn't know him would comment sarcastically about Mike's appearance. He'd just flash a big grin and say, "Hey, that's all right. I've got cancer. But I can deal with it."

During those two years of ministry, Mike courageously loved kids for Christ. Despite his pain and despite his appearance and other physical barriers, Mike went to his mission field and shared himself and the gospel. Mike knew that God had called him to reach teenagers in New Orleans, specifically at Abramson High School, and nothing was going to stop him while he had breath.

A few months after Mike's death, some of his close high school friends, his "club kids," decided to have a special meeting to remember their fallen hero. They wanted to make sure that their classmates understood Mike's message and what had moti-vated this young missionary. The house was packed for the meeting, which began with a slide show of Mike in action—walking on campus, leading games in Campus Life meetings, and just hanging out with kids. Next, several students shared how Mike had touched their lives. Then everyone was invited to share remembrances of Mike. After a dozen or so stories, the high school principal stood and spoke. With tears streaming down his cheeks, he told how he was affected by Mike's courage and commitment.

Mike O'Hara knew Christ, and he knew what God had called him to do. He is a powerful example of Christian courage.

Imagine yourself sitting in Mike's place or, like Thomas, imprisoned because of your faith, or in the place of others whose stories you have read in this book. What do you think you would have done? What will it take to surrender fully to God and to doing his will?

The Contagious Power of Courage

Mike O'Hara's courage is proof that when we have surrendered ourselves to the all-encompassing care of an all-knowing God, that same God gives us the ability to accomplish his all-loving purposes, even when that ability is beyond what we ordinarily think ourselves capable of.

Stories like that inspire. When we hear or read about how a Christian is backed against the wall, our ears perk up. Our eyes refuse to blink. When that same Christian experiences God's amazing grace, we embrace that story with both arms. When we are reminded

When we are reminded of how simple trust in the Lord leads to heroic results, our faith muscles flex.

of how simple trust in the Lord leads to heroic results, our faith muscles flex.

Like new life that emerges from a rotting stump in a forest, courage grows out of the adversity that has taken its toll on others. This is illustrated in the life of the apostle Paul. His lengthy résumé chronicles more than career history; it is the profile of a persecuted saint. Shipwrecks. Stonings. Slander. Beatings. Imprisonment. Ultimately, Paul died bearing on his body the marks of a martyr.

In a letter that Paul wrote from a prison cell to the Christians in Philippi, he refers to the fact that his sufferings have been a source of increased courage in the lives of those who have observed his hardships. Philippians 1:12–14 states, "Now I want you to know, brothers, that what has happened to me has really served to advance the gospel. As a result, it has become clear throughout the whole palace guard and to everyone else that I am in chains for Christ. Because of my chains, most of the brothers in the Lord have been encouraged to speak the word of God more courageously and fearlessly."

Something about another believer's courage in the face of suffering serves to motivate us to access (and even magnify) the courage God makes available to us. The VOM video *Faith Under Fire* tells about Linh Dao, a Vietnamese girl whose father, an underground pastor, had been imprisoned for his faith. Ten-year-old Linh, her mother, and her little sister missed him very much. Every day, Linh made a scratch on her bookcase to keep track of the days her father was gone. Before her dad was put in prison, she was just a child with normal childhood concerns. Nothing more. She didn't need to worry about anything.

But life changed dramatically when her dad was taken from her. Linh recalls, "I prayed every day and every night. My faith grew very fast. I knew one thing I had to concentrate on, and that was spending time learning from the Bible, so when I grew up, I could be like my dad, sharing and preaching."

One day Linh came home from school and couldn't believe her eyes. There was her daddy, healthy and free. It was the most incredible surprise she had ever had.

"I ran and gave him a big hug," Linh says. "We were very happy. I wanted to yell and let the whole world know that I wasn't scared of anything because God always protects each step I take in my life."

Not scared of anything? Those are big words for a young girl. And those bold words were spoken long before she knew the kind of courage she would be called on to exhibit. Linh went on to become the youth leader for a home church. As the leader, she was taken to the police station ten to twenty times. Once, the authorities questioned Linh all day, from 8 A.M. to 5 P.M., for five consecutive days. She was not given any food and was not allowed to go to school. They demanded to know the names of the young people in the youth group and the nature of the youth group activities.

Linh reacted as we might expect. She was fearless. Having experienced firsthand the kind of courage the Holy Spirit had given her father during his imprisonment, her faith remained strong. The green shoot grew from the stump of her father's suffering.

"Why do you waste your time?" Linh asked the police officer. "You know what we do. We do good things. We train youth not to be alcoholics and not to commit crimes."

God desires to release that kind of courage in the life of every believer, not just those in Vietnam. Every country has battles, challenges, and spiritual resistance to those who desire to honor God's truth.

The Courage to Take a Stand

Richard Wurmbrand used to tell the story of when he was a four-teen-year-old in Romania. A friend took him into a bordello. The young Wurmbrand was so ashamed and so frightened that he ran away as fast as he could. He knew he was in a place of danger. As he looked back from the vantage point of many years, seeing his own vulnerable image silhouetted against the backdrop of his vivid memory, he wondered why no priests, pastors, or Christian laymen were picketing the entrance to such houses of perdition. Why weren't courageous Christians boldly taking a stand, stopping every teenager and telling of the risks to the soul?

In his book *Alone With God,* Pastor Wurmbrand wrote:

In the free world, it is customary during a strike for men to picket the entrance to a factory. They often use violence to keep from entering workers who choose not to join their actions. Likewise we Christians must decide to boycott hell, picketing the entrance with determination. . . . We must learn to picket. We must surround hell with a cordon and simply not allow the communists to enter in. If they insist, they can enter the abyss only by stepping over our dead bodies. Our opposition should be that strong. God will not abolish hell if we think like this. If he had none, his laws would not be authoritative. But perhaps it will remain empty. (p. 76)

Even though the Holy Spirit is the one who equips us with courage, and even though the courage he gives us is ignited by the examples of courage we see in the lives of those who bravely stand up to suffering, courage is not automatic. We can't take credit for the valor we have evidenced at times in our lives; neither can we take it for granted. Courage is not an involuntary response—we have to intentionally release it. And that means not retreating or running for cover when courage is needed.

Sadly, a growing number of evangelical Christians appear to be willing to sit on the sidelines instead of taking a stand against sin and for Christ. We need to realize that promotions of immorality are attacks on our Savior.

When recently have you been reluctant to take a stand for the truth and for what you know is right? What held you back?

And a Little Child Shall Lead Them

During the Communist rule in Romania, a Christian woman and her school-age daughter were thrown into jail for protesting the arrest of their pastor. All the prisoners were upset to see the little girl subjected to the demands of incarceration. This unnatural sight troubled even the prison director. "Take pity on your child," he told the woman. "Give up being a Christian, and I'll let you both go free."

The woman struggled with the offer. She loved her Lord, but

she loved her daughter too. Thoughts of what awaited her innocent offspring haunted her. Reluctantly, she called for the prison director and agreed to deny her faith if that would prevent her child from having to suffer. They both were set free.

Within two weeks the Communists arranged for a formal renunciation ceremony. On a stage before ten thousand people the woman was forced to shout, "I am no longer a Christian!"

As they left the gathering, the little girl tugged at her mother's coat and said, "Mommy, I don't think Jesus is satisfied with you today." The child's words cut to the heart. The woman attempted to explain to her daughter that her actions were rooted in love. Looking into her mother's eyes, this little one exhibited wisdom and courage that could only have come from her heavenly Father. She said, "I promise if we go to prison again for Jesus, I will not cry."

The mother could not contain her emotion. She was overcome with joy and pride as well as conviction over her cowardly weakness. Crying out to the Lord for ability that was beyond her own strength, she went back to the prison director and retracted her denial. With a pounding heart but unwavering words she said, "You convinced me to deny my faith for my daughter's sake, but she has more courage than I have."

Both the mother and daughter were returned to prison, and, as she had promised, the little girl did not cave in to her fears.

Facing Our Fears

Courage is not the absence of fear. It is being afraid and still doing what must be done, what God has called us to do. Having courage is not being fearless, it is being faithful—being willing to act despite our fears. That's the mark of godly courage.

On a recent trip to China, a VOM courier met with several believers. Only one of them admitted to being afraid: a twenty-six-year-old woman who holds illegal Christian meetings in her home. She could be arrested for allowing the meetings and could even lose her home, but she faithfully opens her home each week.

When asked if she was ever afraid, she answered, "A little." Then, when she was asked what would happen if she were discovered, she said, "We don't even want to think about that!" Yet the meeting continued.

The host there explained that the woman was afraid because she had not yet been arrested. He added that when she was arrested and found God faithful in trying times, then she would no longer be afraid. His point was that this woman would, through her experiences and by stepping out in faith, gain the courage that was so evident in the other believers. Many of them had been arrested, questioned by police, and even imprisoned. During those difficult times, they had found God to be faithful; therefore, they had become bold in their witness.

Being a courageous Christian begins with the decision to do what God wants, regardless of the cost or our feelings. Next, it takes prayer, asking God for his direction and strength. Then, when we step out in faith, even in a relatively minor conflict, we will experience God's presence and strength. This will help us take the next step.

Courageous Christians act in faith, knowing their calling, depending on God and his love, and empowered by his Spirit. Will you join these heroes?

Sowing Seeds of Courage

- Think of times when you exhibited a measure of resolve and bravery. What risks did you face? Think back to what you were feeling. What evidence did you see of God's faithfulness?

- What situation do you now face in which you know you should make a courageous stand for Christ? With whom can you share details of this situation, asking him or her to pray for you and to hold you accountable?

- In the case of "Thomas" the imprisoned pastor, courage was illustrated by his tenacity. He returned from being beaten to continue his sermon. In what Christian cause did you at one time invest yourself to which God would have you return? Whom can you call today to indicate your desire?

- Courage is definitely enhanced by exposure to the bravery of others. Determine to read through the book of Acts this week. Ask God to give you a sanctified imagination to experience the apostles' hardships vicariously. But don't stop there. Pray for those in other countries who are experiencing firsthand what you're reading about in the Bible.

- God is looking for courageous Christians who will support the cause of the persecuted church. If the stories in this book spark your faith and fuel your courage to make a difference for Jesus' sake, write to The Voice of the Martyrs at P.O. Box 443, Bartlesville, OK 74005, or e-mail them at thevoice@vom-usa.org. They will send you a free monthly newsletter that will help you pray more effectively for persecuted Christians and provide you with practical ways to get involved and help Christians in restricted nations.

CHAPTER 5

Endurance

The Long Haul

They're not especially gifted.
They're just in it for the long haul,
that's all.
Heroes don't quit.
They are marathon runners
who won't walk away
from what they agreed to do.
They complete what they start,
though their feet may stumble.
When they fall, they are humble enough
to brush themselves off
and bury their pride
and regain their stride once again.
Heroes pace themselves by facing the fact
that they come from a long line of finishers
who cheer them on
from the bleachers of eternity.

BY GREG ASIMAKOUPOULOS

THE CRUELTY OF THOSE WHO HATE Christians is all-consuming. More than fifty years ago, a teenage girl working with Richard and Sabina Wurmbrand in the Romanian underground church came under scrutiny. The Communist police discovered that she was secretly spreading copies of the New Testament and teaching children about Christ. After contemplating how they might respond to behavior they viewed as inflammatory, they decided to arrest her. But arresting and imprisoning her on the spot didn't seem nearly harsh enough. They looked for a way to make her punishment agonizingly painful.

Upon further investigation they discovered that she was soon to be married. Heartlessly, they decided to delay her arrest a few weeks, until her wedding day. As the day of her wedding dawned, the authorities prepared to carry out their clandestine plot. Without knowledge of what lay in store, this young bride-to-be dressed in a beautiful gown she had dreamed of wearing all her life. It was the most wonderful, joyous day of her life! Suddenly, the door was pushed open and the secret police rushed in.

When the bride saw the secret police, her response surprised her would-be captors. She extended her arms as if to welcome the handcuffs. Refusing to appear caught off guard, the police roughly clamped the manacles around her wrists. After giving her devastated groom a knowing glance, she kissed her chains and said, "I thank my heavenly Bridegroom for this jewel he has presented to me on my marriage day. I thank him that I am worthy to suffer for him."

Wearing her wedding dress, she was dragged off. Her Christian family and friends wept as they watched the surreal events play out in front of them. They attempted to comfort a heartbroken bridegroom struggling to maintain his composure. He had reason to be concerned. He knew what happened to young Christian girls in the hands of Communist guards.

Five years after that fateful day, the bride-to-be was released. No longer wearing the beautiful gown in which she was last seen, she no longer boasted the beauty she once had. She stood before her family looking thirty years older. Her body was broken, but not her will or spirit. She had held on to a dream that had not shattered. So had her groom. He had waited for her. He said it was the least he could do for his Christ.

That poignant portrait is taken from the pages of *Tortured for Christ*, the classic book on the persecuted church written by the founder of The Voice of the Martyrs (VOM), Richard Wurmbrand. In this story we see the endurance of both the one imprisoned and the one denied his bride.

One of the recognizable fruits of heroic faith is an indomitable spirit. In the fertile soil of fully surrendered hearts, endurance and perseverance ripen and grow. Those who have willingly submitted to the Lordship of Christ and embraced the process of discipleship have developed spiritual stamina.

The Process of Perseverance

Before trusting Christ as his personal Savior, Minucius Felix was a third-century advocate in Rome. Looking back on his experiences before and after his conversion, he hypothesized about how endurance is developed. Felix wrote, "Our mind relaxes through luxury but is strengthened by frugality. . . . To feel and suffer pain is not punishment—it is warfare. Stamina is strengthened by misfortune and often instructs us in virtue. . . . In critical moments, God weighs the character so that our true selves are revealed" (from *Day by Day with the Early Church Fathers*, Peabody, MA: Hendrickson Publishers, 1999, p. 128).

Although he no doubt learned it firsthand, Felix's claims are hardly original. Two hundred years earlier the one credited with writing, under the inspiration of the Holy Spirit, the majority of the New Testament reflected on how his own sufferings had resulted in godly character. In his letter to the Christians in Rome, the apostle Paul describes how perseverance is developed in the life of the believer. He identifies it as a process.

"Not only so, but we also rejoice in our sufferings, because we know that suffering produces perseverance; perseverance, character; and character, hope. And hope does not disappoint us, because God has poured out his love into our hearts by the Holy Spirit, whom he has given us" (Romans 5:3–5).

> **"Endurance only comes as we allow God, through his gracious sovereignty, to take us through difficulties."**

Conner Edwards of VOM attests to Paul's experience:

Endurance only comes as we allow God, through his gracious sovereignty, to take us through difficulties. We have heard the analogy of endurance to training for a marathon. In Jeremiah 12:5 we read, "If you have raced with men on foot and they have worn you out, how can you compete with horses? If you stumble in safe country, how will you manage in the thickets by the Jordan?" That verse is key to understanding perseverance. If we are not willing to embrace the trials in our life today at work, home, school, and so forth, how can we embrace the big trials that may seem more spiritual to us? If we cannot handle the daily stresses of life, how can we deal with them if we feel we are being called overseas to be a missionary? God will entrust us with much more and we will be able to endure the bigger trials he is training us to endure.

Conner's right. In a marathon, anyone can buy a new running outfit, cheer when the gun sounds, and begin the course. But only those who are in shape will finish, or even run for very long. After a few miles, participants are grateful that they went through the arduous (and often painful) process of building up their endurance potential.

What distinguishes long-distance track-and-field heroes is their ability to finish strong—they have prepared well. Likewise, members of the persecuted church around the world have developed the capacity to endure. As they have legged it out with hardship and hurdled over suffering, they may stumble, but they never lose their stride. They consistently stand up to the degrading spittle, the deadly stones, and the dreaded scars of those who mock, imprison, and torture them.

Modern Christian heroes in Eastern Europe, China, Indonesia, Pakistan, and Palestine are spiritual marathoners. Although they may never have heard of an early church father named Tertullian, they share his view from the cell of suffering. He said we dishonor God when we try to avoid the difficult challenges he places in our path.

In your spiritual biography, when did you live as though life were a sprint instead of a marathon? What would it take for you to get in shape spiritually, to build endurance?

The Marathon Quest

Those who are being persecuted for their faith are not the only ones who are candidates for crossing the finish line of faith with a strong stride, however. Several summers ago, veteran missionaries were honored for nearly a half-century of selfless service on behalf of crosscultural evangelism. As part of the ceremony of celebration, they were presented with a plaque that likened the call of God to a marathon race that requires a lifetime to run. The inscription read:

When God calls, a gun sounds, and a marathon begins. A life of service. A lifetime of measured steps which (because of the distance to be

covered) take in stride the potholes along the way. Disappointment.
Tears. Rejection. Exhaustion. Failure. Loss. A cross I think he called it.
The One who finished first, who near the end of his own long-distance
race (though winded) sighed "I thirst!" It was what he saw beyond the
finish line that bade him stay his course. A faithful finish. And his
Father's proud "well done!" It's true. Persistence has its price tags. But
also its rewards! Like the rush that comes when you run through the
pain and find a second wind (when you want to cash it in). But don't
forget the hush. That's another joy in the marathon quest. That quiet
contentment that steadies your steps on "a long obedience in the same
direction." The knowledge that you're being true to what God called
you to do and to that which you promised you would.

Along the way, you've had opportunities to learn endurance and
in the process make a difference for Christ and his Kingdom. Because
of your determination to not give up or in, there are those through-
out this nation (and beyond) who have heard the call of God and
joined the race. You've paced yourself well, and now as you find your
full stride, would you allow us to run at your side? After all, what
you've attained is the goal that we seek. Strong, not weak. Strong, not
wilting. Not bailing out, but holding out to the end. Perseverance.
Persistence. Going the distance. Finishing well.

The same tribute could have been used to celebrate all those
heroes of the faith whose names are recorded in Hebrews chapter
11. Look at that chapter again. It's a list of individuals. Different
races, different professions, different circumstances. Not all were
persecuted, but all experienced the long-distance dimension of

faith. All, having persisted, went the distance and finished well. So did Richard Wurmbrand.

At the age of ninety-one, this faithful advocate for the persecuted church breathed his last breath on earth and stepped across the threshold of heaven. His fragile frame bore witness to the suffering he had endured as a young pastor. Near the end of his earthly trek he was weak and wrinkled. But Pastor Wurmbrand had stayed the course and, by the grace of God, had finished well. For him, life this side of heaven was a laboratory in which God was teaching him the science of learning from suffering and learning to be satisfied with God alone.

The Joy Is in the Journey

As was stated earlier, this is not a laboratory limited to only those who have a prison record or scars on their back. Registration is open to all who desire to live with the same intensity and focus.

Peter Matson was a Swedish immigrant who felt called by God to leave his new homeland of America in order to share the good news of Jesus with the people of China. As he left by ship from San Francisco in the 1880s under the auspices of the Evangelical Covenant Church of America, he began his own marathon. Upon arriving on the Chinese mainland, he adopted the dress and culture of the Asian people he hoped to reach. Facing resistance and being misunderstood, he determined to make friends and earn the right to be heard. Much to his disappointment, nothing of significance happened. Young Peter Matson became "old man" Matson before he had the privilege of baptizing his first convert. Thirty years after setting foot on foreign soil, the baton of faith was successfully passed. But Peter maintained his focus and allowed his disappointments, heartaches, and homesickness to develop a capacity to persevere.

That same spirit of perseverance explains why a couple like Dave and Mitzy Shinen could spend their entire adult lives on a remote island in the Bering Sea. Their goal was to translate God's Word into a previously unwritten language so the indigenous people of the Arctic could hear God speak in the dialect of their heart. Just imagine making a commitment that would consist of more than three decades. Yet that same pattern is repeated in places like New Guinea, Indonesia, and Mexico.

In thirty-plus years as a biographer with Wycliffe Bible Translators, author Hugh Steven has researched and interviewed scores of missionaries. What he has learned is consistent with what church historians have postulated for centuries. Amid the stressful and enduring process of doing what God has called you to do, it is the "doing of the task" that brings fulfillment.

As he approached retirement, Steven decided to channel a lifetime of lessons he had learned as a missionary and a writer into a book that would help Bible translators tell their own stories of heroism, faith, and God's faithfulness. In *The Nature of Story and Creativity* (Santa Ana, CA: self-published, 2001), he explains how the endurance of missionaries about whom he had written (and which he had also experienced firsthand) illustrates a principle he'd long been aware of as a writer. Steven draws parallels between what makes for effectiveness on the mission field with what makes for effectiveness in a good novel.

He writes, "I believe it's the journey with all its surprise, danger and all its challenges for risk and choice that reveals the true essence of an individual. In a word, the journey is the story because without the journey there could be no goal" (p. 91).

"In a word, the journey is the story because without the journey there could be no goal."

This reality is not limited to Bible translators who invest thirty-five years of their lives to finish a New Testament project. It also applies to pastors of small churches around the world who maintain their stride as they approach the finish line of the race God has called them to. In addition, blue-collar workers, teachers, business executives, and homemakers have discovered the joy of the journey and the personal pride that is found in perseverance. What Richard Wurmbrand modeled through fourteen years behind bars is accessible to every believer. No matter our occupation or the nation in which we live, we all can finish strong. But it demands keeping our eyes on the goal.

Paul wrote about *his* race toward the finish in Philippians: "But one thing I do: Forgetting what is behind and straining toward what is ahead, I press on toward the goal to win the prize for which God has called me heavenward in Christ Jesus" (3:13*b*–14).

In a marathon, runners who lose sight of the goal can become distracted and discouraged. With lungs bursting and legs aching, each stride becomes a struggle, and they consider dropping out. But those who keep the goal in sight gain encouragement and strength to push, to give their all. They finish strong!

As you consider your life's "race," what threatens to hinder your view of the finish line, to distract you from looking toward "God's prize"?

Frankly, when Paul wrote to the believers in Rome about properly interpreting their less-than-ideal circumstances (Romans 5), he was writing to ordinary, everyday disciples without theological training or advanced education. They were people very much like us. Very much like a woman by the name of Esther Palmer.

Pointing the Way

Esther attended an upper-middle-class Presbyterian church near her home in Southern California. It was a thriving church where the gospel was preached and 50 percent of the budget went to the support of missions. It also had a great youth program for the Palmers' two sons.

Esther took her faith seriously. She loved attending adult Sunday school and a neighborhood Bible study. She enjoyed serving on one of the church's several missions committees. By virtue of her pastor's heartbeat for global Christianity, Esther learned of the plight of the persecuted church. She became aware of the kind of tireless endurance that marked their heroic faith. Little did she realize that before her life was over she, too, would be challenged to endure hardship by exhibiting a similar kind of dependence on the Lord.

As Esther entered her thirties, she began to suffer from rheumatoid arthritis. As the disease manifested itself throughout her body, her symptoms increased in severity. Each day became a living hell. As one of Esther's friends put it, she was dying by inches.

Esther sought sanctuary among her friends at church, but just getting there became a challenge. Her body was becoming stiff. Her agility disappeared. Her fingers became permanently curled and her knees permanently locked. Esther could not turn her neck. On top of being for the most part immobile, her body was wracked by excruciating pain.

At first Esther felt sorry for herself. She threw a daily pity party, but usually she was the only one who showed up. But through the encouragement of a couple of close friends in her Bible study group, she chose to accept her difficult challenge as part of God's plan for her life. In much the same way as the martyrs she had heard about at church, she endured suffering as a soldier of the cross. Esther maintained her discipline of daily devotions. Because her husband was dealing with challenges of his own, she often felt as though she was on her endurance course all by herself. But building upon the pain of the past, she proved she could endure.

Curiously, the index finger of Esther's right hand did not curl up toward her palm like the others. It remained a rigid pointer that she could use to punch buttons on a touch-tone phone. And Esther used that one straight finger to the glory of God. As a member of the church's Refugee Resettlement Committee, she volunteered to be telephone chairperson. With that one finger she contacted agencies and solicited donations of furniture, clothing, and household items. She even arranged committee meetings. Esther discovered that, in spite of her limitations, she had value. She realized that even though her body was mostly dead, all she needed was an index finger to stay in the race. And fixing her eyes on Jesus, she ran "with perseverance" until the day she died (Hebrews 12:1).

If you ever meet a believer who has suffered as a Christian or for being a Christian, you discover something very interesting about him or her. The person's scars (be they physical or emotional) have become like badges of honor that he or she wears with pride. The reason is the "joy in the journey" that the person has experienced thanks to the invisible presence of God. A presence that attends those who endure no matter what the cost. Just ask To Dinh Trung and Li Dexian.

Case Studies in Endurance

Because of his faith, To Dinh Trung was sent to prison in Vietnam for a six-month sentence, leaving his wife and small children at home. Once inside the prison, he shared his faith with other prisoners and saw several come to Christ.

Three months into his sentence, VOM published his name and address, resulting in thousands of letters sent to the government urging his release from prison. Surprised by the international outpouring of support for this simple tribesman, the authorities offered to let him go home. Much to their surprise, To Dinh Trung refused the early release—he had seen many people come to Christ in prison, and he wondered who would disciple these new believers if he were to leave. He decided that it was more important to help them send their roots deep into the faith than to enjoy the comfort of his home and to be reunited with his family. So he endured, joyfully, the last three months of his sentence in order to better serve God and build his church.

Even as these words are being written, another courageous Christian, Pastor Li Dexian, is locked up in China. When he is asked how many times he has been arrested, he simply shrugs his shoulders—it has been so many times that he has lost count. But the smile on his face reveals his feelings. He's not counting arrests; he's counting on Christ. He's not worried about the police; he's concerned about helping Christians to mature in their faith. He doesn't want to talk about the arrests; he wants to discuss God's blessings.

"Persecution is a king of blessing," he says. "When we came to Christ, he gave us a new life. Persecution is a part of that new life."

Pastor Li and other persecuted believers don't worry about persecution. They don't dread it, nor do they revel in it. They simply accept struggle and suffering as part of the new life that Christ purchased for them with his blood. It comes with running the race.

Li could easily escape persecution. He could move to a different city where police do not know him so well. He could hand over the church leadership to others and take a less conspicuous role. He probably could even leave the country, for the Chinese authorities would be happy to rid themselves of such a "troublemaker."

But Li keeps on. The authorities shut down his large gathering of believers, thinking that would end the work. They closed one large church, but forty smaller house churches have sprung up to take its place. Li often visits these smaller churches, encouraging believers to keep on, to endure in the faith. His message is simple: Do what I do. Keep serving Christ, regardless of the cost or of what any human may do to you. When the arrests come, praise God for the new people you can reach in prison with God's love.

If we want to have endurance, we can't simply change our environment each time things grow difficult. In America and other free nations, changing the environment is often easier than dealing with an issue and keeping on with our effort. But sometimes God calls us to stay in a place and work for him, regardless of whether it is easy or comfortable to do so.

Endurance is not glamorous; it does not offer high praise or huge rewards. The Olympic 100-meter dash champion is far better known than the marathon winner. One is called the "world's fastest," while the other is barely mentioned in the sports pages.

Often those around us encourage us to give up, to move on, or to change the scenery. Move out of that tough neighborhood where your witness is so desperately needed. Give up on that marriage that doesn't magically meet all of your needs. Stop witnessing to that person who has rebuffed your talk of Christ. Don't mention church to that friend who turned down your invitation. Others say give up. God says keep on.

Others say give up. God says keep on.

Endurance is not a gift that a person can develop in one day or even in one season. You can't wake up one morning and decide to hang in there. No, endurance is the result of a lifetime of simple acts of obedience.

As you look back over the past several years of your Christian life, what have you done to develop your endurance? What is God telling you to "keep on" doing for him at home, in your community, or at work?

It Comes with the Turf

Paul, our veteran endurance coach, has made it quite clear that "everyone who wants to live a godly life in Christ Jesus will be persecuted" (2 Timothy 3:12). Paul wrote those words from prison, awaiting his execution. Knowing his earthly race is ending, he shares profound and poignant advice. As the aging apostle bears his heart to Timothy, his young protégé, he does not sugarcoat the conditioning program that is required of those who would finish the marathon of faith.

In the world-famous Boston Marathon, runners know what to expect. Near the end of the twenty-six-mile race they are confronted with notorious "Mile Nineteen." This stretch of the course is particularly grueling because it demands that the runners inch their way up a relatively steep incline. Those who know the racecourse know what's coming. They can pace themselves. If we are convinced we will face our own "Mile Nineteen," we can anticipate and allow the process of endurance to get us ready.

Young Timothy had barely begun to tie the laces of his running shoes when Paul called him to learn from the laps he had already completed. He cautioned him to expect rejection as a Christian, but he also invited him (and us) to anticipate God's intervention.

> You, however, know all about my teaching, my way of life, my purpose, faith, patience, love, endurance, persecutions, sufferings. . . . Yet the Lord rescued me from all of them. In fact, everyone who wants to live a godly life in Christ Jesus will be persecuted, while evil men and impostors will go from bad to worse, deceiving and being deceived. But as for you, continue in what you have learned and have become convinced of, because you know those from whom you learned it. . . . (2 Timothy 3:10–14)

Paul knew better than to expect Timothy to be motivated by his example alone or his teaching. Endurance, like courage, is not the fruit of human invention. Trying really hard to be like another or giving your all to do your best isn't sufficient to pass the test of persecution. And so Paul, without even stopping to dip his quill in the ink bottle, continued to write:

> . . . and how from infancy you have known the holy Scriptures, which are able to make you wise for salvation through faith in Christ Jesus. All Scripture is God-breathed and is useful for teaching, rebuking, correcting and training in righteousness, so that the man of God may be thoroughly equipped for every good work. (2 Timothy 3:15–17)

As motivating and inspiring as stories of heroic faith may be, the example of another is not ultimately what will allow us to endure the persecutions to come. It is what we discovered a couple of chapters ago. Nothing can replace the Word of God.

Coaches are critical, but the conditioning manual is far more important. Go back and review the stories of men and women who endured terrifying captivities. You will see how much they depended on the Bible. God-breathed words became the means of their spiritual stamina.

What does it take to build endurance, run the full race, and finish strong? We have seen that it begins with conditioning, preparing for life's major challenges by meeting the small ones, and feeding on God's Word. The process continues as we follow the example of those who have run the race before us, finding positive role models and mentors. And it concludes triumphantly as we keep focused on the finish line, our goal, God's prize.

Conditioning Tips for Spiritual Marathoners

- Endurance is a process. We gain increased stamina from situations that God allows us to go through. As Paul wrote in Romans, each one builds upon another. Think back on your own life. In your journal, record how your ability to endure difficult situations is traced to trials that are part of your track record.

- List two or three challenging situations that you need to work through right now, where you need to persevere. Think of someone who can hold you accountable for meeting those challenges. Imagine that person as your personal spiritual trainer.

- What would you be able to sing from memory if held as a captive? Is your repertoire of hymns and worship songs very extensive? One way to increase your retention of Scripture and lyrics is to buy some CDs of Scripture songs. Play them as you drive to work or work around the house. It's amazing how easy it is to memorize verses that are set to music.

■ What do you anticipate will be your "Mile Nineteen"? (For example, health issues, financial concerns, relational conflicts, and so forth) What can you do *now* to begin to prepare for that point in your life so that you can finish the race successfully?

■ Perhaps you are experiencing a major struggle right now (for example, difficulties in your marriage, conflicts with teenagers, a moral dilemma at work). It most likely isn't overt persecution for your faith, but it is challenging your ability to endure. Don't try to handle this alone. If you do not have someone to confide in and pray with, don't continue your solitary confinement. Reach out to someone and solicit his or her friendship and prayer support. Whom will you ask to do this for you?

CHAPTER 6

Obedience

A Way of Life

Heroes do
what God asks them to.
They act in accordance
with what he demands.
It stands to reason.
For heroes, obedience
has no off-season.
It's a way of life.
Heroes stand out
by always being about
their Father's business.
As a prophet once said
to a conniving old king,
"What sings most beautifully
is not bleating lambs
about to be sacrificed,
but a life that is quick to obey."

BY GREG ASIMAKOUPOULOS

WITHOUT ONE WOMAN'S DETERMINATION to fully obey what she believed the Lord was demanding, The Voice of the Martyrs ministry might never have begun. The man God had chosen to be his spokesperson for the persecuted church might never have spoken up. Richard Wurmbrand credits his wife with finding his voice.

This Lutheran pastor and his wife, Sabina, were attending the "Congress of the Cults" in Romania. More than four thousand pastors, priests, and ministers from every imaginable denomination had gathered in 1944. After electing Joseph Stalin as the honorary president, delegate after delegate approached the podium proclaiming that Christianity and Communism essentially embraced the same ideology. The common message was one of mutual co-existence. "We can all get along side by side!"

Sabina was dying a slow death inside. "These people are spitting on the face of Jesus," she told her husband. "Go wash the shame off his face."

In his heart Richard knew what the consequences would be if

he publicly countered the sentiment of the assembly. "If I speak against the Communists, you will no longer have a husband," he whispered to his wife.

With steely eyes she stared at her pastor-husband and said, "I do not wish to have a coward for a husband."

Her comment caught him by surprise, but it was what Richard Wurmbrand needed to be reminded of—the cost of obedience he owed his Savior. Getting up from his seat, he moved to the front of the convention hall and addressed the four thousand delegates. He challenged them to resist the rising tide of accommodation that in essence would mean disregarding the Great Commission.

When righteousness is held hostage behind enemy lines, you do whatever is necessary to set it free.

This act of obedience proved costly. On that day Pastor Wurmbrand took his first steps toward unthinkable torture and a total of fourteen years in prison. But both Sabina and Richard knew they had no option. When godless men make the rules, the rules are made to be broken. When righteousness is held hostage behind enemy lines, you do whatever is necessary to set it free.

In even a cursory reading of Scripture, the words *obedience* and *obey* stand out:

- So if you faithfully obey the commands I am giving you today—to love the LORD your God and to serve him with all your heart and with all your soul—then I will send rain on your land in its season, both autumn and spring rains, so that you may gather in your grain, new wine and oil. I will provide grass in the fields for your cattle, and you will eat and be satisfied. (Deuteronomy 11:13–15)

- It is the LORD your God you must follow, and him you must revere. Keep his commands and obey him; serve him and hold fast to him. (Deuteronomy 13:4)

- To obey is better than sacrifice, and to heed is better than the fat of rams. (1 Samuel 15:22b)

- But from everlasting to everlasting the LORD's love is with those who fear him, and his righteousness with their children's children—with those who keep his covenant and remember to obey his precepts. (Psalm 103:17–18)

- Now reform your ways and your actions and obey the LORD your God. Then the LORD will relent and not bring the disaster he has pronounced against you. (Jeremiah 26:13)

- The LORD thunders at the head of his army; his forces are beyond number, and mighty are those who obey his command. The day of the LORD is great; it is dreadful. Who can endure it?. (Joel 2:11)

- [Jesus] replied, "Blessed rather are those who hear the word of God and obey it." (Luke 11:28)

- "If you love me, you will obey what I command." (John 14:15)

- For it is not those who hear the law who are righteous in God's sight, but it is those who obey the law who will be declared righteous. (Romans 2:13)

- Therefore, my dear friends, as you have always obeyed—not only in my presence, but now much more in my absence—continue to work out your salvation with fear and trembling, for it is God who works in you to will and to act according to his good purpose. (Philippians 2:12–13)

- As obedient children, do not conform to the evil desires you had when you lived in ignorance. But just as he who called you is holy, so be holy in all you do; for it is written: "Be holy, because I am holy." (1 Peter 1:14–16)

- We know that we have come to know him if we obey his commands. (1 John 2:3)

Clearly, God's clarion call to his children is *obedience*. He wants us to understand what he wants; then he wants us to do it. It's as simple as that. Those with heroic faith take God seriously and do what he says.

Obedience is not a gift or a God-inspired trait. It is a *choice* that we must make every day. Obedience contains no "ifs" ("If this happens, then I will obey"). When obedience leads to trouble, a hero has the faith to know who will lead him or her safely through the trouble. Heroic Christians do not have to be brave or fearless; they have to believe God and then act on that belief with obedience, totally depending on him.

What God Wants

Obedience to God has powerful implications for every aspect of our lives. God revealed his will for us in his moral law, epitomized in the

Ten Commandments. Jesus summarized the law and highlighted its importance with this statement: "'Love the Lord your God with all your heart and with all your soul and with all your mind.' This is the first and greatest commandment. And the second is like it: 'Love your neighbor as yourself.' All the Law and the Prophets hang on these two commandments" (Matthew 22:37–40).

Then, just before returning to heaven, Jesus left his disciples with this admonition: "All authority in heaven and on earth has been given to me. Therefore go and make disciples of all nations, baptizing them in the name of the Father and of the Son and of the Holy Spirit, and teaching them to obey everything I have commanded you. And surely I am with you always, to the very end of the age" (Matthew 28:18–20).

So if we are determined to obey God, we must continually ask, "Do my actions express love for God and my neighbor?" and "What can I do to bring the Good News of Christ to others, to make disciples?"

That's how heroic believers live, in every nation. In fact, those who are persecuted, tortured, and killed for their faith are attacked because of how they live, because they obey God, regardless of the consequences.

The Drumbeat of Obedience

Obedience to God was the cadence to which Richard and Sabina Wurmbrand marched. Throughout their lives they answered to a higher court than public opinion or ungodly laws. On many occasions Christians in the West called Pastor Wurmbrand to task for his willingness to smuggle Bibles across closed borders. This man, who distinguished himself as a faith hero through a determination to be a person of obedience, had no qualms about disobeying the laws of certain countries that prohibited the distribution of the Bible.

For Pastor Wurmbrand, it really was an issue of all being fair in love and war. God's love is the highest authority, and those who war against it are not in a position to tell those who obey God what they can and cannot do. In a book entitled *Where Christ Still Suffers* (Gainsville, FL: Bridge-Logos Publishers, 1984), Richard wrote, "What is highly immoral according to common standards becomes an act of love if it results in the salvation of men. If God gave his Son to die for this purpose, we also feel justified in sidestepping some of the norms of ordinary Christian behavior. We smuggle the Word of God to those who hunger for it in order that God's creatures in other lands might enter heaven. Some say that to do so is immoral. We consider it immoral to leave souls without the Word of God. Would you consider it immoral to help starving children because a government forbids them aid? Is not food for the soul as important as food for the body?"

Disobedient Disciples

For the person who is consumed with a desire to do what is morally right, disobedience to a civil law may be required in order to fulfill the mandate of a sacred law. We saw that in the bold behavior of Peter and John in Acts chapter 4. When the Jewish leaders arrested them and commanded them to quit preaching about Jesus' resurrection, the twosome didn't back down. They stood up and said, "Judge for yourselves whether it is right in God's sight to obey you rather than God. For we cannot help speaking about what we have seen and heard" (Acts 4:19–20).

In the very next chapter, we see others taking their cues from Peter and John. The Lord was powerfully using the whole company of spirit-empowered disciples in the lives of common people. Many were being healed, and the Word of God was being declared with unusual results. As Luke indicated in the sequel to his gospel, the acts of the apostles were a continuation of the life-changing ministry that Jesus began prior to his ascension. ("In my former book, Theophilus, I wrote about all that Jesus *began to do and to teach* until the day he was taken up to heaven. . . . "—Acts 1:1–2, italics added) For those who received what the apostles offered, it was indeed as if Jesus himself were still ministering in their midst. Through the Holy Spirit, Jesus was still at work.

In response to the apostles' popularity, the Jewish high priest had Jesus' followers arrested. Because they had not obeyed the ordinance to keep their mouths shut about the Rabbi from Nazareth (made clear in chapter 4), they would have to suffer. But here's where it gets interesting. God sent an angel to unlock the prison door and set the apostles free. In addition, the angel was told to pass on important instructions: "Go, stand in the temple courts . . . and tell the people the full message of this new life" (Acts 5:20).

Clearly, this passage authorizes Christians to disobey civil authorities in order to be obedient to God. As the rest of chapter

5 develops, we see the freed apostles back at it, both in the city streets and the temple courts, "as they had been told," not by the Jewish leaders, but by the messenger of God. When arrested a second time, the apostles were called on the carpet before the Sanhedrin. Though they were not jailed again, they were flogged before being released. But did they obey the Jewish law? No way! Luke's description is priceless: "The apostles left the Sanhedrin, rejoicing because they had been counted worthy of suffering disgrace for the Name. Day after day, in the temple courts and from house to house, *they never stopped* teaching and proclaiming the good news that Jesus is the Christ" (Acts 5:41–42, italics added).

Christians often ask how they can determine God's will. That certainly is a worthy pursuit, for we wouldn't want to live outside his will. Yet much more problematic is how we live when we *do know* what God wants and how he desires us to live. And we don't have to worry about the authorities harassing us or imprisoning us. Unfortunately, we find it easy to rationalize our disregard of God's clear commands. "Love God" . . . "Love your neighbor" . . . "tell the world" . . . it couldn't be more clear.

Long-Distance Obedience

About five decades after the incident reported in Acts 5, John encountered a young disciple of Jesus by the name of Polycarp. Realizing the young man's potential, the aging apostle poured his life into him. Polycarp later became Bishop of Smyrna (what is now Izmur, Turkey). The potential that John had seen was fulfilled with great effectiveness. Polycarp's singular focus and extraordinary faith channeled into believers around the Roman Empire through his sermons and letters.

Unlike many believers who died premature deaths while suffering for their faith, Polycarp was able to avoid being apprehended. At the impressive age of eighty-six, the old man was still defending the faith. The bishop was en route to a distant town when some young boys recognized him and proceeded to inform the resident Roman soldiers. When the soldiers found Polycarp enjoying a meal, the bishop offered to share his food.

After eating together, the soldiers demanded that the old man go with them. He prevailed on their mercy and asked if he could have an hour to pray. The soldiers agreed. Later, they reported that the intense passion of the bishop's audible prayers moved them to a sense of their own need of God and Christ's forgiveness for their sins.

"For eighty-six years I have served him. How then should I blaspheme my King who has saved me?"

Eventually, Polycarp was taken to the governor of Rome. Despite Polycarp's age, Caesar's appointee sentenced the bishop to be burned at the stake in the middle of the city. Moved perhaps by his winsome personality or his feeble physical state, the governor offered Polycarp the opportunity to recant his faith in Christ in exchange for his life. Polycarp's response was living (and dying) proof of his lifelong obedience: "For eighty-six years I have served him. How then should I blaspheme my King who has saved me?"

Tradition suggests that the soldiers bound Polycarp to a large stake and positioned chopped planks of wood at his feet. Once lit, the flames engulfed the brave bishop, but, miraculously, did not even singe a hair on his body. The governor, refusing to be thwarted, ordered a soldier to thrust a sword into Polycarp's side. The blood that gushed from his body ended his life and, ironically, doused the fire.

This disciple had demonstrated the same devotion and compliance as the unstoppable apostles. When he realized that the governor's sentence would be the final word in his life's story, Polycarp prayed: "I praise you for making me worthy to be received among the number of the martyrs this day and this hour, so that I share in the cup of Christ for the resurrection of my soul."

The Fight for Freedom Is Far from Over

Polycarp's story is moving and dramatic, but beatings, bloodshed, and torture are still taking place over the issue of religious freedom. On every continent of the earth, there are Christians who would rather obey God and honor him (by openly worshiping and evangelizing) than obey dictates that demand otherwise. Sadly, their stories are often untold or unread. To the degree that they are made public, they may also receive public shame or worse. Yet, they have an amazing willingness to submit to the will of God, to obey him rather than people.

These courageous men and women have discovered what François Fénelon, a French Christian mystic in the seventeenth century, believed—that "peace and comfort can be found nowhere except in simple obedience" (*Let Go,* New Kensington, PA: Whitaker House, 1973, p. 9). Even though their obedience may be accompanied by suffering, tears, or broken dreams, these believers, who bend the knee to God, are not bowed down by the injustices they are forced to endure. Within their hearts they stand tall, validated by the Holy Spirit. They routinely taste flavors of God's grace they didn't even know existed.

These who exhibit such heroic faith can do more than teach us how to disobey prejudicial or ungodly laws of the government in order to live with unbridled obedience before the Lord. They can also teach us how to say no to the carnal dictates of our convenience-driven hearts. The reason is clear. It is the willingness to bear the inner cross of self-denial that explains why some dare to do what others fear while refusing to do what others give in to.

The Ultimate Example

The greatest act of obedience is *not* witnessed by many and certainly not publicized. It is the allegiance that is pledged in the crucible of the tempted heart. When Jesus approached the destination of his incarnation, the cross cast a shivering shadow across his only-too-human apprehension. Kneeling against the gnarled stump of a dead olive tree, the Savior candidly confessed his fear. He didn't want to endure the excruciating torture of Roman crucifixion. But that wasn't the half of it.

Jesus didn't want to embrace what only he was capable of wrapping his sinless arms around. He knew what the Cross was really about. Far more than a long, painful death, it represented a dance with the devil that would result in spiritual separation from his Father. For Jesus, that was worse than suffering or human death. So the Son of God drew back from the unimaginable suffering that he would bear as he absorbed the sin of all people of all times. We can't even begin to imagine the heinous torture that kind of vicarious suffering represented. But Jesus was quite capable of imagining it. That is why, in the prayer recorded in the Gospels, we hear Jesus pleading with his Father: "May this cup be taken from me" (Matthew 26:39).

In his words, we hear Jesus' humanity and vulnerability. Nevertheless, Jesus does not compromise. Taking a deep breath, he says, "Yet not as I will, but as you will."

Clearly, Jesus understood what Fénelon experienced more than sixteen hundred years later. Fénelon wrote, "We can add to our God-given cross by agitated resistance and unwillingness to suffer. This is simply an evidence of the remaining life of self. . . . The resistance within is harder to bear than the cross itself! But if you recognize the hand of God, and make no opposition to his will, you will have peace in the midst of affliction" (*Let Go,* p. 3).

That's it! That explains what we have seen in the lives of so many faith heroes in this book. Like Jesus and Fénelon, they have discovered the senselessness of trying to will their own way and resist the affliction that obedience often attracts. Once you "take up your cross daily" and die to yourself, you have no reason not to be bold when it comes to refuting the lies of a society or a culture bent on spitting in Jesus' face. By shouldering the cross, we find the grace of the Holy Spirit that cushions the weight and gives us contentment.

When the writer of the epistle to the Hebrews suggested that

Jesus "learned obedience from what he suffered" (5:8), he wasn't inviting a debate about whether the Son of God lacked certain divine knowledge when he came to earth. Jesus obviously had no need to learn anything. As the only begotten of the Father, his knowledge was complete. But knowledge remains abstract until it is tested by experience. Since spiritual obedience is a uniquely human quality, only as a human could the Son of God be tested on his knowledge.

What the writer of the letter appears to be suggesting is that suffering was the teacher that tested the perfect student. A "crucifixion" took place within the heart of Jesus before the one on Calvary. While encountering Satan in the Judean desert and while praying in the Garden of Gethsemane, he suffered. Scripture says the sorrow was so intense in the garden that he actually was sweating blood (Luke 22:44). That spiritual suffering and surrender resulted in obedience to the Father's plan and brought about the physical suffering on a literal cross.

Obedience is never an act of the human will; it is linked to the eternal perspective we looked at in chapter 1, grounded in faith in the goodness of God and the ultimate destination of our earthly journey. Remember what Hebrews 12:2 says? It was the joy that Jesus knew awaited him in heaven that allowed him to stare down his momentary doubts and obey the Father's will. He knew that the ultimate joy was part of a will that (by definition) can only be wonderful.

Hannah Whitall Smith was not immune from suffering in her life during the latter half of the nineteenth century. Splinters of "the daily cross" were imbedded in her shoulder. Yet, as one who found obedience a worthwhile task, she wrote, "The will of a good God cannot help being 'good'—in fact, it must be perfect; and, when we come to know this, we always find it 'acceptable'; that is we come to love it. I am convinced that all trouble about submitting to the will of God would disappear, if once we could see clearly that his will is good. We struggle and struggle in vain to submit to a will that we do not believe to be good, but when we see that it is really good, we submit to it with delight. We want it to be accomplished. Our hearts spring out to meet it" (*The God of All Comfort*, New Kensington, PA: Whitaker House, 1997, p. 79).

"I am convinced that all trouble about submitting to the will of God would disappear, if once we could see clearly that his will is good."

So maybe that's what it comes down to, why we're reluctant to obey God. Perhaps we aren't really convinced that he is good and that his way is best. The only solution for this dilemma is to take another look, a close look, at what God has done in the past. Reread the biblical accounts of God's gracious acts on behalf of his people. List his promises of a bright future for those who follow him. And gaze again into the eyes of his Son, who willingly laid aside heavenly glory, became a tiny speck in his magnificent creation, lived as a tempted and tested human being, and experienced incomprehensible torture and pain . . . for you. Then you will see that God is good and can be trusted.

Obedience That Death Cannot Silence

Perhaps no one person has used his pen to challenge the underground church more than Dietrich Bonhoeffer. His call to both godly obedience and civil disobedience certainly qualifies him as a person from whom we can learn about heroic faith.

Like Wurmbrand, Dietrich Bonhoeffer was a Lutheran pastor whom God used in remarkable ways during World War II. This gifted communicator is often associated with *The Cost of Discipleship*, a book he wrote in the 1940s. Those who know his story would attest to the fact that he had firsthand knowledge of that cost and was willing to pay it with the currency of obedience.

Dietrich announced his desire to become a minister when he was only fourteen years of age. His wealthy and influential father ridiculed the idea. As far as the elder Bonhoeffer was concerned, the church was apostate. Young Dietrich said he wanted to be a voice within it to help reform it. When he was only twenty-one, the young Bonhoeffer completed his theological dissertation called *The Communion of Saints*. It received praise from readers beyond those who taught at the university he attended. He was on the road to reach the reforms that he had promised his father he would effect.

In 1933 Adolf Hitler rose to power in Germany. Hitler convinced the state Lutheran Church to adopt a clause in its bylaws that would prevent anyone with Jewish ancestry from being ordained to ministry. Like Richard Wurmbrand, Bonhoeffer was a lonely public voice of opposition. As he did when he was fourteen, Bonhoeffer vowed to be an instrument of redemption within the church. He did what Pastor Wurmbrand did and sowed the seeds of a church that would germinate underground.

Through his sermons, correspondence, and published articles, this twentieth-century Martin Luther repudiated the cowardly compromise he saw among his colleagues. He courageously opposed the evil Nazis and attempted to raise his voice on behalf of those victimized by Hitler's subtle strategy to create a superrace.

In April 1943, Bonhoeffer's reforms were slowed when he was arrested in Berlin for "subversion of the armed forces." But his obedience to God's call to protest sin in the church and society was not derailed. He may have been behind bars, but his sentence did not mean persuasive thoughts would no longer flow from his pen. With only his life to lose, he did not hold back in his rebuke of Christians who remained silent when they should have cried out.

Two years after being imprisoned, Bonhoeffer was moved to the Flossenburg concentration camp, where he was executed by hanging on April 9, 1945. Only two weeks later the Allied Forces liberated the facility where the obedient pastor had breathed his final breath. Although it might seem like a cruel joke that Bonhoeffer would be denied freedom by only a few days, his martyrdom has motivated a host of daring Christians to pay the cost of discipleship, perhaps more than if he had survived.

The camp doctor at Flossenburg who witnessed Bonhoeffer's last moments before his death would later describe a moving scene. The pastor, humbly resigned to a fate his prayers had not avoided, knelt in prayer before being led away to the gallows. According to that nameless physician, he had "hardly ever seen a man die so entirely submissive to the will of God."

Those who choose to obey God, to shoulder their cross and follow their Savior, know that God is good and that living his way is the only way.

Prerequisites for Cross Carrying

- What evidence do you have of God's goodness (in Scripture, from the testimonies of others, and so forth)? What personal evidence do you have? What keeps you from fully trusting him?

- Sabina Wurmbrand was the one who challenged Richard to obey the Lord and take up his cross (even though it would require prison). Who in your life has earned the right to challenge you to take up your cross when they see it gathering dust in a corner? Ask them to sit down with you and evaluate your public "obedience quotient."

- When it comes to your private "obedience quotient," no one can score your progress as you can. Right now, what do you believe God wants you to do? He may be telling you to turn from a destructive habit, to come to the defense of someone who has been wrongfully accused, to share the gospel with a neighbor, or to selflessly serve your spouse. What will you do to obey him (your obedience plan)?

■ What excuses do you find yourself making to avoid obeying God? Keep the list nearby and use it as a reminder to make no excuses.

■ If you are approaching the age of Polycarp, write a lengthy letter to each of your grandchildren. Describe in it how you became a committed follower of Jesus. Offer advice to them for resisting temptation. Express your desire for their lives.

CHAPTER 7

Self-Control

The Going Price

They know what it means
to hold their horses
or their tongues
or hold their ground
when the claim they've staked
for righteousness
sounds foolish
to the crowd.
Heroes pay whatever price
the going rate requires.
The loss of their job.
The loss of their reputation.
The loss of their life.
But what heroes surrender
they're willing to give.
That's why it's called sacrifice.

BY GREG ASIMAKOUPOULOS

IT WAS THE DAY THE PLIGHT of the persecuted church overseas arrived in America. After the simple question "Do you believe in God?" was answered in the affirmative, a trigger was squeezed and a Christian teenager died. On this dark April day when the world refused to rhyme, a pastor scribbled the following lines in his journal, attempting to put the feelings of a shocked nation on paper.

In a not-so-little town on the Front Range of the Rockies, a room designed for learning became a tomb for those gunned down. There were bullets and blood and a reign of terror followed by a flood of fear. Wearing black trench coats to hide their insecurities, two boys in men's bodies lived out the violence they'd previously caged in their minds. It's a nightmare that has left us blind with rage and grief. And for those who've lost loved ones, there is no relief. It's the kind of tragedy we never dreamed would strike in our own backyard. It's hard to explain how and why, but we try 'cause we must, while we simply trust that a loving God is weeping with us and remains in complete control. When push comes to shove, bullets fly and children die. And when hearts break, we feel the ache and reach out to those left alone.

The date was April 20, 1999. Twelve students and a much-loved teacher were gunned down at Columbine High School in Littleton, Colorado. At least three of the slain students were born-again Christians. Their outspoken testimony had made them targets for the two teenage terrorists, Eric Harris and Dylan Klebold, who took their lives.

As CNN broke into regularly scheduled television programming, millions of disbelieving Americans attempted to come to terms with the unthinkable horror. Parents were confronted with the reality that sending kids to a neighborhood school does not guarantee safety. They dug deep within themselves to try to find the means to cope. They struggled to find a way to explain this seemingly senseless tragedy to their own children.

The Cost of Dying

Seventeen-year-old Rachel Scott arrived at Columbine High that Tuesday morning in time for her 7:20 class. She was a bit more tired than normal because Monday had been especially long. In addition to working after school at the local Subway sandwich shop, she had attended her youth group at church. Nonetheless, Rachel was looking forward to what she thought would be a typical day.

This pretty and petite high school junior viewed school as more than just a place to learn. It was a place where she looked for ways to share her faith in God with her friends and peers.

Rachel was young, but she took her relationship with Christ seriously. In her journal she regularly recorded her desire to express her faith in tangible ways.

One such entry expressed disappointment that the very people she wanted to reach for Christ turned away from her: "I've lost all my friends at school. Now that I've begun to walk my talk, they make fun of me. . . . I am not going to apologize for speaking the name of Jesus. . . . I will take it. If my friends have to become my enemies for me to be with my best friend Jesus, then that's fine with me. Ya know, I always knew that part of being a Christian means having enemies, but I never thought that my 'friends' were going to be those enemies" (*Rachel's Tears*, Nashville, TN: Thomas Nelson Publishers, 2000, pp. 96–97).

Rachel continued to reach out to her fellow classmates who didn't understand her devotion to Christ. In *Rachel's Tears*, a book about their heroic daughter, her parents, Darrell and Beth, write, "Rachel loved God and she had an overpowering urge to communicate that love to everyone she knew. She didn't beat people over the head with her Bible and she never coerced anyone into faith. Instead, she shared her faith by living her life to the full, praying that others would see the divine light that burned so brightly in her heart."

Exactly a year before she died, Rachel's journal entry confessed her uncompromising commitment to be God's person wherever she was, no matter what it might

"She shared her faith by living her life to the full, praying that others would see the divine light that burned so brightly in her heart."

cost her: "I am not going to hide the light God has put into me. If I have to sacrifice everything, I will" (p. 97).

A month before she was martyred for admitting that she believed in God, Rachel's unwavering faith was evidenced when she wrote that she dared to believe that she could "start a chain reaction through acts of kindness and compassion" (p. 169).

When faced with the muzzle of a terrorist's gun, Rachel did not flinch. When provided an opportunity to deny her Lord, she refused. Knowing what was required to start a chain reaction of Christian commitment in her world, she did not cave in to her unavoidable fear.

A person who is self-controlled will make sacrifices to achieve the desired goal. An athlete trains vigorously in order to perform well on the field. A soldier endures basic training and intense preparations to be ready for battle. An artist spends years honing and perfecting skills. A heroic Christian gets rid of anything extraneous to obey the Lord. Rachel was willing to "sacrifice everything," if necessary, to live for Christ. Think, for a moment, of what your faith has cost you. Are there certain sacrifices you know you should make but have not? What will it take to give up those things that stand between you and the Savior?

Rachel Scott chose to pay the necessary cost. So did a frail twenty-two-year-old woman from North Vietnam traveling by train to Ho Chi Minh City.

The Cost of Living

The difficulties she had endured in only two decades of life masked her once-youthful face. Stress and hard work had taken their toll. But this amazing individual had accomplished what most people three times her age haven't.

As she sat upright on the hard wooden seat for three consecutive days, she recalled with humility what the Lord had allowed her to do for the sake of God's kingdom. Single-handedly, she had planted three separate Christian congregations. Being the only mature believer in her region, she had won person after person to Jesus by simply sharing her story and calling for a personal commitment.

This young woman didn't have access to a car or even a bicycle, but she had strong legs and arms. For that she could thank the Lord. They had enabled her to walk great distances to meet with people or paddle a small wooden boat to her church meetings. But her strong arms and legs were weary from nonstop ministry. Her entire body was exhausted.

Though unable to lie down on the seat, she did manage to nod off for stretches of time while sitting up. It's quite possible that as she slept she dreamed of the inhumane abuse that she had been subjected to. The local police routinely tried to intimidate her with threats. Others harassed her. Even her parents protested against her activities. As Buddhists, they could not understand their daughter's passion to talk about and worship Jesus. It's also probable that she dreamed of those in her three congregations who had asked her to go searching for copies of God's Word. They were so hungry to know more about Jesus.

The weak and weary traveler was jostled awake by the erratic bouncing of the train as it headed in a southbound direction on uneven tracks. She was anxious to reach the end of her eight-hundred-mile trek, hopeful that her trip would be a success and that she would be able to find the spiritual nourishment her flock so desperately needed—and wanted.

Upon reaching the city formerly known as Saigon, the haggard young woman hoped she could find just one believer who would be able to help her. The city was big, and she felt a bit insecure. She took comfort in knowing that her congregations were praying for her safety and success. Their prayers were answered. This woman pastor was directed to Christians from the West who had arrived in Ho Chi Minh City with all the Bibles she needed. They also purchased a bicycle so she could travel with less difficulty between her parishes. Her heart was overwhelmed.

Before seeing her off at the train station, the Christian "tourists" gathered around this dear sister and prayed God's blessing on her ministry. As she boarded her rail car, the whistle blew and the train began to pull out of the station. New friends waved at one another, friends who had come to realize that they were, in reality, members of an eternal family. The long, lonely journey that would take another three days would not seem as lonely.

Two young women. Two very different stories. But one common thread. Each girl accepted her plight in life willingly and not reluctantly. Both were very much in control of the circumstances that resulted in the loss of life or the loss of youth. Both Rachel Scott and the unidentified Vietnamese church-planter walked into the opportunities God provided them with their eyes wide open.

Self-control means having the personal discipline to do what you know you must do, to focus on the task at hand, avoiding all distractions. Consider a small child, for example, who has been told by his mother to get something from his room and bring it to her. On the way, however, he becomes distracted by the family puppy and then by a toy that he sees in the hallway. Soon he forgets his mission entirely until sharply reminded by Mom. We expect that kind of behavior from children, but we become frustrated and even infuriated when we see it in adults. Gaining self-control and discipline should be part of growing up, something we learn as we mature.

Yet, believers often become distracted in their spiritual walk. They know what they are to do and are highly motivated to do it, but soon they turn aside to other pursuits. In contrast, those with heroic faith keep at the task until it is finished. Nothing could keep the woman from North Vietnam from doing what she knew God wanted her to do. She had self-control; she was disciplined.

How easily are *you* distracted from doing what God wants? What interests tend to distract you from commitments you have made? What can you do to avoid those distractions, to resist those temptations?

Maintaining Control While Giving His Life

Perhaps you have heard the expression "Not to decide is to decide." In other words, when you are faced with a dilemma, you can be proactive and take the initiative, or you can be reactive and let others decide for you. Those really are the only two choices: to be intentional or unintentional.

"Not to decide is to decide."

Heroes choose to be intentional. They

know the risks associated with their call. They act in accordance with what they feel God wants them to do. And once they make a decision, they accept personal responsibility for their actions. This kind of self-control is yet another one of the traits of those who are known by their heroic faith.

Based on the example of Jesus, we know that mature self-control can result in personal sacrifice (as was true of Rachel Scott), or it can result in willingly doing what the situation calls for instead of running from it or becoming distracted (as was true of the young Vietnamese pastor). The Savior maintained his sense of purpose and demonstrated an amazing sense of timing. At times he, after healing someone, insisted that the object of his touch not reveal his identity. At other times he didn't seem to mind. One time he purposely avoided going into Jerusalem (even though his enemies were expecting him). But then, on his last visit to Jerusalem, he knew what awaited him and yet "turned his face as a flint" toward the city, walking into the trap of the traitor.

Jesus grew weary of the disciples' pettiness—they would routinely argue about who was the greatest. He despaired of their apparent inability to understand—often they would appear mentally dense. But Jesus chose to stick with them. He even stomached their personal stench as he stooped to wash their feet. That was a servant's job. But Jesus sacrificed his pride to do what needed to be done. Jesus angrily overturned tables in the temple and took a whip to the moneychangers, but when struck in the face by the mocking soldiers, Jesus practiced what he had preached to his followers and turned the other cheek.

Like the Vietnamese girl, he lived two lifetimes in one in order to provide for the spiritual needs of those who depended on him. Like Rachel Scott, Jesus was willing to let an assailant take his life because avoiding it would have broken the chain reaction of grace that would reach around the world. He knew when to show restraint and when to boldly take a stand for righteousness.

For Jesus, self-control was the key. John 10 records Jesus' painting a self-portrait. His brush strokes are bold, yet the emerging details reveal a pastoral scene. Jesus is a good shepherd who will do whatever is necessary to provide for the spiritual welfare of his flock. In a veiled reference to the Pharisees, Jesus distinguishes himself from those who only feign concern. He is quick to say that he will lay down his life for the sheep. But in verses 17 and 18, Jesus makes it quite clear that what he is willing to do (and that which he is planning to do) will only take place on his timetable. He remains in control of his options. "The reason my Father loves me is that I lay down my life—only to take it up again. No one takes it from me, but I lay it down of my own accord" (John 10:17–18).

Whereas Jesus owned responsibility for choices that were his alone to make, those who are entirely surrendered to him claim a similar "response-ability." Their ability to respond to others' demands is based in confidence that the worst action anyone can ever take against them is to take their life. With that eternal perspective bringing the present situation into focus, they choose to believe they always have choices. They choose to believe that circumstances do not control their options (no matter how threatening or intimidating they may be) . . . just like one older woman who willingly chose to sacrifice the joys of marriage for a higher calling.

The Motives of Being a Martyr

In the mid-1980s a dear Chinese woman approaching retirement age acted with amazing self-control and confidence. She was moved with compassion for believers within her country who had no access to God's Word. With the help of The Voice of the Martyrs (VOM and others), she was able to distribute forty thousand Bibles. This woman knew what the consequences of her action would be if she ever were apprehended—passing out Scripture portions was against the law—but that did not deter her. To understand this courageous woman's passion to distribute God's truth, you just needed to ask her husband. He would attest to her sold-out commitment.

When the police identified who had been illegally smuggling the Bibles, they attempted to arrest the woman. But before they could nab her, she was able to escape. For seventeen years she has been hiding from the police who continue to look for her. As a result of this woman's desire to put the needs of fledgling Christians in China above her own needs or those of her family, she is able to see her husband only about twice a year (VOM newsletter, May 1994).

The kind of sacrificial commitment that issues from pure motives and a giving heart is rare. The rise in terrorism has called attention to countless acts of "martyrs." But those deaths—suicide missions—are the very antithesis of self-control.

As September 11 demonstrated, Islamic terrorists are willing to become human bombs that kill Western Christians. In their minds we are infidels and instruments of Satan. Christian beliefs that celebrate human equality (for example, in Christ there is no male or female) fuel the wrath of those who insist that women's faces be covered and their rights reduced to those of chattel.

Trainers of al-Qaida militants teach them that by killing us they will become instant martyrs. They believe that upon blowing themselves up—and as many "infidels" as they can in the process—they will immediately go to Paradise. But that is not the whole of the logic. They are also motivated to sacrifice themselves by what they have been taught awaits them. According to these recruiter-teachers, each martyr will be given seventy young virgins with whom he will be free to enjoy limitless sexual pleasure.

The Chinese Bible smuggler is willing to deny herself physical pleasure and companionship. And for what purpose? To provide nourishment for Christians hungering for God's Word. Her acts of sacrifice serve an end that serves others and not herself. The Islamic militant is willing to do physical harm and unthinkable destruction in order to feather a love nest in the afterlife with the realizations of his X-rated fantasies.

We have seen that Jesus knew when to show restraint, and that disciplined believers to deny themselves to further the cause. Restraint and self-denial are increasingly uncommon in a culture that promotes a smorgasbord of options for self-indulgence. And those promotions are so difficult to resist as they entice us with materialistic dreams, sexual fantasies, and culinary delights—trappings of "the good life."

Yet, the cost of discipleship includes denying ourselves as we follow Christ. Which of these self-indulgence options do you battle? How do they threaten to pull you away from your Christian walk? What can you do to become self-disciplined in the areas of money, possessions, food, and sex?

Staying on the Altar

The apostle Paul provides helpful clarity to this discussion. In his letter to the Romans, he applauds the concept of sacrificial commitment, referring to the act of mature faith as "a living sacrifice."

> Therefore, I urge you, brothers, in view of God's mercy, to offer your bodies as living sacrifices, holy and pleasing to God—this is your spiritual act of worship. Do not conform any longer to the pattern of this world, but be transformed by the renewing of your mind. Then you will be able to test and approve what God's will is—his good, pleasing and perfect will. (Romans 12:1–2)

Although the apostle is not referring to literal martyrdom, he is addressing the death of a person's carnal nature. Unlike the assertions of the al-Qaida teachings, living (or dying) in order to please one's bodily desires is the antithesis of God's desire in this life (or in the life to come). Instead, believers are called to surrender themselves as on an altar of sacrifice. The backdrop Paul assumes is the sacrificial system of the Old Testament in which goats, lambs, and bulls were slaughtered by the priests and presented to God as an offering for sin.

But since this surrender of the human ego is spiritual and not literal, Paul makes it quite clear that we are to take the initiative and do what is necessary to align ourselves to God's purpose. This requires a change in the way we let the culture dictate our desires. It requires a proactive approach to feeding our mind with God's truth. Unless we do whatever is necessary to deny ourselves (rendering our egos as dead), we will revert to our tendency to follow self-serving appetites. As Jay Kesler would often say, "The problem with living sacrifices is their tendency to crawl off the altar."

"The problem with living sacrifices is their tendency to crawl off the altar."

Workers with The Voice of the Martyrs have thought much about the concept of voluntarily laying down our lives while maintaining the ability to respond to circumstances proactively and not reactively. Conner Edwards writes, "Self-control and sacrifice are fundamental to the Christian life. As we grow in our faith and see that God is who he says he is, our willingness to obey his call to 'deny ourselves and pick up his cross' becomes a part of our lives. We know we have a choice to either pick up our cross and deny ourselves or deny the cross and embrace ourselves. The one choice brings life and the other death and destruction, although the path to life comes at a great cost."

Eugene Peterson's paraphrase of the first two verses in Romans 12 brings out the nuances of what it takes to embrace a life of purposed choices and guarded options: "So here's what I want you to do, God helping you: Take your everyday, ordinary life—your sleeping, eating, going-to-work, and walking-around life—and place it before God as an offering. Embracing what God does for you is the best thing you can do for him. Don't become so well-adjusted to your culture that you fit into it without even thinking. Instead, fix your attention on God. You'll be changed from the inside out. Readily recognize what he wants from you, and quickly respond to it. Unlike the culture around you, always dragging you down to its level of immaturity, God brings the best out of you, develops well-formed maturity in you" (*The Message*).

Rachel Scott demonstrated that quality of maturity despite her age, as did the Vietnamese woman on the train. It's the maturity that the Chinese woman had as well. All three knew what God desired and then acted accordingly at the appropriate time. They were fully aware of what being a living sacrifice would require, yet they placed themselves on the altar in the center of God's will.

Conner Edwards continues, "No one has exemplified this principle better than our persecuted brothers and sisters in Christ. They know that following Christ may cost them seeing their families because their ministry may take them away from their family weeks at a time or may cause their imprisonment for months and even years. Many of the persecuted have denied themselves promotions at work and even a better education in order to follow Christ. They know such things are temporal, but the kingdom is eternal. As we look at the persecuted, we can learn much from their sacrifices."

God promises many benefits to those who are willing to sacrifice their rights, relationships, or their very lives. But unlike the terrible situations where men and women are taught to hate and to kill by blowing themselves up in acts of terror, God promises that for which the human soul longs. We were created for more than the momentary pleasure of physical intimacy. Our heavenly Father offers those who acknowledge his Lordship a peace that passes all understanding and joy during trials. And that's just in this life. In the world to come we will know the uninterrupted joy of endless worship as we gather before his throne with those who will be there as a result of our witness and sacrifice.

Believers with heroic faith are self-disciplined. They make sacrifices, avoid distractions, practice restraint, and choose to act. How does your faith measure up?

What It Takes to Follow the Good Shepherd

- To get a better understanding of sacrifice, choose one activity or pursuit that tends to slow you down in your pursuit of God. Sacrifice it for a week and use the time to further Christ's kingdom.

- To better understand how easily a person can become distracted, during a short trip in the car, keep track of possible distractions that might tempt you to veer away from reaching your goal (for example, sale at a store, fast-food snack, a friend's house, scenery, etc.). Later, review your list and look for parallels in the Christian life. That is, what could be a "fast-food" distraction in your walk with Christ? Or what might be a relational distraction? And so forth.

- To help you learn restraint, fast for a day, devoting mealtimes to prayer. Or have a TV fast for a week.

■ It's conceivable that you could be asked (like Rachel Scott) to lay down your life one day. But the judgment of "dying daily" is every Christian's life sentence. What is God challenging you to "lay down" for him today?

■ This chapter includes two poignant examples of women who suffered greatly to deliver God's Word to those who didn't have it. Whom do you know who might benefit from having a copy of the Bible? Go to a Christian bookstore and buy that friend a copy. Before presenting the Bible to the person, ask God to open his or her heart to your visit.

CHAPTER 8

Love

A Hero's Flight

Have you ever wondered
what allows heroes to soar
high above the plains of mediocrity?
Or what it is in heaven's name
that enables them to swoop so low
to pick up the downtrodden.
Just what is it that gives them lift
to carry those who've lost the will to fly?
It's the breeze that blows from God's own heart
that propels a hero's flight.
It's nothing less than selfless love.
That's the wind beneath their wings.

BY GREG ASIMAKOUPOULOS

IN 1982, CHARLES COLSON, the convicted-Watergate-criminal-turned-Christian-head-of-Prison-Ministries, boarded a plane for a speaking engagement. On the same flight was Benito Aquino, an exiled political journalist from the Philippines. Aquino recognized Colson and excitedly approached him. He introduced himself and with much passion described how he had become a Christian by reading *Born Again* (an autobiographical account of Colson's prison experience and conversion).

Aquino detailed how he had been a victim of injustice under the dictatorship of Ferdinand Marcos. His journalistic influence had called into question Marcos's unethical regime. As a result, he had been imprisoned for seven years and seven months. Aquino confessed how much he had despised God and his oppressors. He had been a hostage of his own hate. As that airline encounter continued, the Filipino exile told how his Christian mother had brought him a copy of Colson's book. He read it and gave his life to Christ. Aquino described it as the turning point in his life.

Upon being released from prison, Aquino had fled to the

United States for sanctuary and had begun to grow in his faith. It was during this time that he met Colson. The "chance" meeting was the beginning of a strong friendship. They traveled together and made public appearances, sharing their testimonies all over the country. One day Aquino confided to Colson that he believed God wanted him to return to the Philippines to pick up where he had left off. This time, however, he was determined to challenge a corrupt government in Jesus' name. Aquino was convinced that the power of Christian love is greater than the power of evil.

"If Marcos lets me run for president, I'll be elected. If he throws me in jail, I'll establish a new chapter of Prison Fellowship. And if Marcos kills me, I'll be with Jesus."

As Aquino prepared to return to his homeland that longed for his leadership, Colson expressed concern over the nation's unrest. He asked his young friend if he had considered what might happen to him. The forty-something visionary said, "If Marcos lets me run for president, I'll be elected. If he throws me in jail, I'll establish a new chapter of Prison Fellowship. And if Marcos kills me, I'll be with Jesus."

Within a few weeks of that conversation, Aquino flew back to the Philippines. As he exited the plane at the Manila airport, what some political analysts had predicted occurred. An assassin's bullet ended young Aquino's life. But amazingly, it did not end his dream. As the Philippines grieved the loss of their outspoken Christian hero, the seeds of love he had sown while still in exile began to germinate.

Cardinal Sin, of the Catholic Church, picked up Aquino's baton and called the nation to repent and believe in Jesus that they might return to their spiritual roots. And they did. Throughout the country a great spiritual movement was sparked by Aquino's aborted return and the cardinal's call to righteousness. Prayer groups and house churches spread throughout the country.

Shortly thereafter, when three hundred troops announced a revolution, Cardinal Sin went on television and called Christians (both Catholics and Protestants) to take a stand against an evil dictatorship. The result was nothing short of miraculous. Two million Filipino people took to the streets, and Marcos's tanks couldn't move. The country's tyrant was overthrown, democracy was restored, and the winds of revival blew through the island nation.

When Chuck Colson told this story to the gathered delegates of Congress '88 in Washington, D.C., he celebrated more than the courage of his fallen friend. He attested to the presence of love in this modern-day hero. It was the overwhelming quality of heroic faith that led to a willingness to lay down his life for others. In Colson's words, "One man of character came out of a jail cell to say, 'I will stand because the power of Christian love is greater than the power of evil.'"

The Supreme Example of Personal Sacrifice

Jesus first observed that the ultimate power of love is released through one who is willing to offer up his life. He said, "Greater love has no one than this, that he lay down his life for his friends" (John 15:13). Jesus was obviously referring to what he would do on the cross to convey his unconditional love for an unrighteous world. But that's not all he was saying. His example provided us with a paradigm by which to evaluate expressions of love and with which to motivate us to follow his lead.

What Jesus lived and what he taught could be summarized in this simple equation: "love to the *nth* degree = 1 life 4 others." If you want to convince another person that he or she matters more to you than you matter to yourself, you give yourself to that person. That is the ultimate payout a person can make. It is why, without thinking twice, a parent will jump in front of a speeding car in order to save the life of his or her child.

This involuntary love that a parent innately has for his or her flesh and blood has been observed in Christian martyrs throughout the ages, whether or not they have children of their own. In fact, those who have been branded as heroes are willing to channel the love normally reserved for family toward those who are more needy than they are. Selfless love that refuses to fade is their telling tattoo. Their feet are calloused from continually following the footsteps of the Savior along the steep paths of the journey into others' lives.

An Unexpected Day of Reckoning and a Heroic Display of Love

On another international trip, a passenger with nowhere near the celebrity status of Aquino took the words of Jesus to heart as he willingly chose to lay down his life for others.

Among the least-known passengers who perished on the *Titanic* was a thirty-nine-year-old pastor from Great Britain.

Those who know his story refer to John Harper as the *Titanic*'s last hero. When this young man of God booked his passage on the maiden voyage of the world's largest ship, he had no idea what lay in store. Reverend Harper had accepted an invitation to hold a series of meetings at Moody Memorial Church in Chicago. After his wife's premature death, he welcomed the opportunity to visit America. He had struggled with sorrow as well as the ongoing issues related to being a single parent. But he had sensed that God was going to use him in a significant way on this trip to America.

Traveling with his nine-year-old daughter and an eleven-year-old niece, Harper was determined to make this extended trip an adventure that all three of them would remember for the rest of their lives. As it would turn out, the well-intentioned pastor's hopes for a memorable trip and his wish to be uniquely used by the Lord would not be in vain. Both desires would be fulfilled, but not in the way he had envisioned.

Long before April 15 was designated as the annual day of reckoning for American taxpayers, that date in 1912 proved to be a day of reckoning of another kind. For believers aboard the *Titanic*, it was their faith in God that was taxed. For those without faith, it was a day when they were forced to come to terms with what they would owe for an eternity.

When disaster struck and the ship began to sink, all of the women and children were given seats in the twenty-one lifeboats. So were men traveling alone with their offspring. But John Harper felt a check in his spirit. The Holy Spirit was challenging him to lay down his life for the sake of others. Not taking the seat in the lifeboat reserved for him would save only one person, but he was sure that he could reach many others for eternity by giving his life.

Harper placed his little girl and young niece safely in one of the lifeboats and remained on the doomed deck of that most famous ship. As he wept and waved good-bye to a daughter that he knew he would not see again this side of heaven, he demonstrated the kind of self-control that distinguishes those with heroic faith. Seeing a distraught man on the ship's deck who had not been able to find a life jacket, the kind pastor gladly gave him his. Moving from person to person among those who had been separated from family members safely placed in the lifeboats, John called on them to trust Christ.

One hundred yards away, the fortunate but heartbroken passengers in the lifeboats watched the *Titanic* begin to sink into the icy black waters of the Atlantic. From their vantage point they could not see the moving scene on the slanting deck. Pastor Harper was kneeling with a group of frightened passengers, leading them in the sinner's prayer. They were not close enough to hear him ask a few of the ship's musicians begin to play "Nearer, My God, to Thee."

John Harper had every right to join the women and children who survived. But, like the heroes of faith we have considered in Hebrews 11, he was not a hostage to instantaneous gratification nor committed to his family at all costs. John Harper bravely chose to stay behind in order to witness to the passengers and crew who would perish with the ship. John Harper's actions were portrayed in James Cameron's blockbuster Hollywood film, but his story of courageous heroism had more drama than the fictional love story the screenwriters wrote into the picture. Even more important, John Harper's decision to lay down his life was not in vain.

John Harper bravely chose to stay behind in order to witness to the passengers and crew who would perish with the ship.

Years later, a Swedish sailor gave his testimony in a Canadian church. Miraculously, this man had survived the *Titanic* tragedy by floating in the frigid waters, wearing a life preserver until another ship had rescued him. The converted Swede credited John Harper with leading him (and others) to Christ while the life-jacket-less pastor treaded water until he succumbed to the icy Atlantic.

Would Benito Aquino or John Harper have wished that their lives had ended differently? Probably not. As a philosopher by the name of Rubin once said, "A life without surrender is a life without commitment." These heroes were joyfully resigned to their fate, knowing they were following Christ up the hill to their own "Calvary." They did not lay down their lives reluctantly but peacefully. Based on what we know to be true about these two men of God, Rubin's famous quote could be adapted to read, "A life without surrender is a life without commitment or contentment."

These two men died contented because their contentment was grounded in their commitment—a commitment rooted in the compelling love of God that Paul describes in 2 Corinthians 5:14: "For Christ's love compels us, because we are convinced that one died for all. . . ." Here the often-persecuted apostle defends himself against those who accuse him of being crazy. Critics thought Paul was "out of his mind" because he was fanatical about his primary goal in life—

to take as many people to heaven with him as he could. When it came to reaching people who needed Jesus, Paul was passionate.

In the sentences surrounding verse 14, the apostle attempts to explain why he feels the way he does and why he does what others bad-mouth him for doing. He says that what God has done on our behalf reminds us that we have reason to "fear" him. The Father did what we could not do for ourselves; he sent his Son to die for the sin of the world. The past has been dealt with. Every human being can become a new creation in Christ. And since that is a possibility, we are called to do what we can to make it happen.

Paul goes on to describe the ministry of reconciliation that believers have been given. God's love as expressed in Jesus must not be limited to a few. When we know what God thinks about those for whom Christ died, we can't help ourselves. His love compels us to color the world with his love (even if that means shedding our blood). His love compels us to no longer live for ourselves but for him and, as a direct result, for others.

Aquino and Harper gave their lives for people they did not know because Christ's love compelled them. They had within them the kind of love that would not let them rest until they had extended the borders of Christ's kingdom and staked a claim for their Savior.

Love Is a Verb

The word *love* is commonly used and discussed as though it is primarily a noun describing an emotion, a feeling—something we find, fall into, or seek. Thus, when hearing admonitions to "love your neighbor" or "love your enemy," we find it difficult to identify. How can we possibly work up a feeling of love for someone we don't know or for those who hate us? However, what we see from Scripture and from the powerful example of Jesus shows that love is first and foremost a *choice* that leads to action. That is, regardless of our feelings, we must *choose* to act in love toward others. Then the feelings may follow.

Aquino and Harper made love-choices: Aquino to go, Harper to stay. As a result, they both gave their lives to save others.

Our love must not be restricted to the lovable—those whose company we enjoy, those who love us. As we reach out in love to those who don't deserve it, we reflect Christ's selfless love. People see the Savior in us.

Think of someone you dislike or someone who seems to be out to get you. What can you do to "love" that person? What choice do you need to make? What action do you need to take?

A Tough Pill to Swallow

Aquino and Harper are not lone examples. They are indicative of thousands in countries too numerous to list who are thought to be crazy because of what they do in the name of love. And within the hearts of those who are willing to lay down their lives for others flows a passion for reaching the world. The hearts of these would-be martyrs pulsate with a love that offers undeserved forgiveness.

That was true of Corrie ten Boom. During World War II, her family expressed their love for God by harboring Dutch Jews in their home. When the authorities discovered their clandestine behavior, the ten Boom family was arrested and sent to prison.

The consequences for their "crime" became all the more cruel when the Nazis separated family members from each other. Against the backdrop of this unimagined nightmare, Corrie and her sister Betsie were grateful to be imprisoned in the same facility, and they thanked God for an unexpected blessing. Sadly, however, they never saw their father again. The eighty-four-year-old man died nine days after being arrested.

Corrie and Betsie were forced to endure inhumane living conditions at Ravensbruck in Germany. Like many persecuted believers, they were tortured and abused by guards and camp officials. Along with six million Jews, Betsie died. Corrie, however, was released by mistake. But she was not entirely released. She was haunted by the prison memories and unloving thoughts toward those who hurt her.

After Europe was liberated, Corrie went through doors the Lord opened for her to travel in America and tell her story. But after a year of itinerant speaking, she sensed it was time to return to Holland. When the invitations came to travel to Germany, she resisted. How could she go back to a place with which she associated so many horrible experiences? She really didn't want to accept the invitations, but in her heart she knew that God wanted her to. So, eventually, she went.

In meeting after meeting Corrie saw people whom she recognized from camps where she had been imprisoned. Among them were some who had tortured her. Feeling resentment rise up within her, she called on the Lord for the ability to love these people. At one particular gathering she saw a man she immediately recognized as one of the guards who had been responsible for the deaths of countless innocent people. When he came up to greet Corrie at the conclusion of her talk, it was apparent that he was now a Christian. Corrie could also tell that he did not recognize his former prisoner. Reaching out his hand, he made reference to how wonderful it is that the Lord forgives.

This was a tough pill to swallow, and Corrie wasn't sure she could get it down. But as she reached out her hand to shake his, what happened surprised her. She was overwhelmed with a love the Lord had given her for this man. She was able to genuinely forgive him. Her obedient choice to reach out led to the change in her heart. As she looked within herself, she knew it was the love of Christ that compelled her to love this man. Even though he had been so cruel to her and so many others, she had to admit that Jesus had died for him as well.

A Love That Refuses to Be Silenced

As has been seen before, the principles of heroic faith are not evidenced only in Holland, Germany, and the Philippines. Heroes compelled by the love of Christ to love their enemies are everywhere. We may marvel at how a Corrie ten Boom could find the ability to forgive someone who unjustly put her in prison, but look around you. Perhaps you know someone who has shown love to one who was justly locked behind bars. That was the case of an American by the name of Wayne Messmer.

Wayne's fame as a Chicago sports personality extends throughout the Midwest. His rich baritone voice is enjoyed by thousands each year who gather in historic Wrigley Field, where he serves as field announcer for the Chicago Cubs. And Wayne brings tears to fans' eyes and goose bumps to their arms as he sings a heartfelt version of "The Star-Spangled Banner." Wayne is also the voice of choice to sing the national anthem at Chicago White Sox baseball games and Chicago Blackhawks hockey games. When not in the press box or on the field, this multitalented man is on a podium somewhere giving a motivational talk. Suffice it to say this born-again Christian makes his living with his voice.

Because of Wayne's unique occupation, what happened in April 1994 left him demoralized. Following dinner with friends in a restaurant after a hockey game, as Wayne was returning to his car, he was shot at point-blank range by two teenage thugs. Because of the nature of the wounds, the doctors who operated on him wondered if he would live. When they were finally able to stabilize him, they prepared his wife for the bad news. Because the bullet had passed through Wayne's throat, it was doubtful that he would ever sing again. But thanks to the prayers of Wayne's fellow believers, family, and friends, Chicagoans witnessed a miracle. Six months later, Wayne Messmer stood before Chicago sports fans and sang the song that is synonymous with his name.

As he sang "Oh, say can you see . . . ," it was plain to see the evidence of a ten-hour surgery that saved his life. What wasn't as easy to detect was what was going on in Wayne's heart. Physical recovery was one thing. Emotional recovery was something else. Like Corrie ten Boom, Wayne struggled with anger and resentment toward his attackers. But because of his faith in Jesus, he was convinced that his complete healing depended on his ability to forgive his young assailants.

In his book, *The Voice of Victory* (WPM Publishing, Inc., 2000, pp. 236–37), Wayne writes, "In spite of my frustration, I believed I had reached a point where I could honestly say that I had forgiven these young men. In doing so, over a period of contemplative and reflective prayer and meditation, I was confident that I had set myself free from the chains that had connected me to the incident."

Although one of the boys had been released on a plea bargain, James Hampton remained incarcerated. For Wayne to prove to himself that he really had forgiven his would-be killers, he drove the 225 miles to the Galesburg (Illinois) Correctional Center and asked to see young Hampton. Although a few years had passed and Hampton was no longer a teenager, Wayne found the strength and grace in his heart to speak these words: "James, I'm here to see how you are doing."

After a two-hour emotional visit, Wayne turned to leave. Reaching out and touching Hampton's forearm, he offered a benediction that revealed the love he felt in his heart: "James, I bid you peace!" The compelling love of Christ was at work once again.

Holding on to resentment and anger is a natural response to hurt and abuse. But God calls us to live differently, to forgive. On the cross, Jesus prayed, "Father, forgive them, for they do not know what they are doing" (Luke 23:34). Forgiveness is not natural—it's *supernatural*, a gift from God. That's what Wayne discovered.

What grudges do you harbor? Whom do you need to forgive?

Forgiveness is not natural—it's *supernatural*, a gift from God.

Serving with Love

Those who love also serve. They take seriously Jesus' words to his disciples just before he left them and walked to Calvary *for* them. After washing twelve pairs of dirty feet, Jesus told these men (his closest followers), "You call me 'Teacher' and 'Lord,' and rightly so, for that is what I am. Now that I, your Lord and Teacher, have washed your feet, you also should wash one another's feet. I have set you an example that you should do as I have done for you. I tell you the truth, no servant is greater than his master, nor is a messenger greater than the one who sent him. Now that you know these things, you will be blessed if you do them" (John 13:13–17).

Sister Kwang took those words seriously in a filthy Chinese prison.

This courageous Christian had been imprisoned for organizing groups of evangelists to travel around China forming small house churches. When Communist officials discovered Kwang's activities, they beat her twelve-year-old son to death. Still, she refused to deny Christ and continued to build the house-church movement after they released her. Finally, in 1974, the Communists decided to make an example of "Mother Kwang," as her church members knew her. She was sentenced to life in prison, placed in an underground cell, and fed only dirty rice.

One day, the prison guards demanded that someone volunteer to clean the bathrooms daily. At first, none of the women prisoners spoke up. But then Mother Kwang stepped forward and volunteered to do the rotten task. She saw this action as obedience to Christ and as an opportunity to share her faith with women whom she would otherwise never see. During her time in that prison, she led hundreds of women to Christ.

Jesus said, "And if anyone gives even a cup of cold water to one of these little ones because he is my disciple, I tell you the truth, he will certainly not lose his reward" (Matthew 10:42). Like forgiveness, selfless service is a love-choice. Mother Kwang chose to clean prison bathrooms. And her washing-feet cup-of-cold-water action led to many finding the Savior.

Where is God calling you to serve, to love others for his sake? Whose feet do you need to wash? Who needs a "cup of cold water" in Jesus' name?

What Love Demands Is Love

Life-giving love. Forgiving love. Serving love. The compelling love of Christ comes in a variety of flavors. Those whose hearts beat with heroic faith are also capable of another kind of love. It's the kind that willingly endures the suffering and tortures that unloving people inflict, simply because these believers are overwhelmed by the undeserved and unconditional love they have received from the Lord. This kind of love motivates believers to go the distance and endure whatever trials come their way as a way of expressing their sold-out devotion to Jesus.

Perhaps that was part of what the apostle Paul had in mind when, in reflecting on his many trials, he told the Christians in Philippi that he could do everything through Christ, who strengthened him (Philippians 4:13). Christ's sacrificial death on the cross gave Paul the motivation to endure, and the Holy Spirit living within gave Paul the power.

When we realize what Christ has done for us and how much he loves us, we want to return that love. We feel "compelled." "For Christ's love compels us, because we are convinced that one died for all, and therefore all died. And he died for all, that those who live should no longer live for themselves but for him who died for them and was raised again" (2 Corinthians 5:14–15).

When we feel like giving up and bailing out, we need to stop and consider what Jesus did for us. The suffering Jesus endured on our behalf had no end. Remembering and understanding what he did inspires a perseverance to keep going and to keep loving in the face of hardship or shipwrecked relationships.

It did for Richard Wurmbrand. When he looked deep into his own heart to try to understand how he had been able to survive all that he went through, he uncovered an answer. He discovered that his endurance was due to his indescribable love for his Savior. That is why he could write the following in *Tortured for Christ:* "If the heart is cleansed by the love of Jesus Christ, and if the heart loves him, you can resist all tortures. What would a loving bride not do for a loving bridegroom? What would a loving mother not do for her child? If you love Christ as Mary did, who had Christ as a baby in her arms, if you love Jesus as a bride loves her bridegroom, then you can resist such tortures. God will judge us not according to how much we endured, but how much we could love. I am a witness for the Christians in communist prisons that they could love. They could love God and men" (p. 39).

It's no wonder that when the apostle Paul harvests the fruit of the Spirit in Galatians chapter 5, the first fruit he holds up is love. Of all the fruit, love is the most significant. All the other fruits flow out of love. The same is true as you look back at the eight characteristics of heroic faith. Eternal perspective, dependence on God, love of God's Word, courage, endurance, obedience, and self-control are all derived from being filled with and compelled by the love of Christ. In the lives of spiritual heroes (wherever they are found), their overwhelming love for Jesus is nothing more (and nothing less) than an automatic response to his love for them. And then that love overflows and spills out to the waiting and watching world.

Will you love for the sake of your Savior and because of the Cross?

Tasting the Various Flavors of Love

■ We all have an appetite for true stories like that of Benito Aquino and John Harper. Their kind of Christlike love that pays the ultimate price inspires and motivates. If you don't already have a copy, get *Extreme Devotion* (Nashville, TN: W Publishing Group, 2002). This daily devotional book written by The Voice of the Martyrs is filled with accounts of self-sacrifice.

■ The thought of literally giving your life for the sake of the gospel may be hard to swallow. But, for starters, begin to chew on this thought: Offering forgiveness to someone who is not sorry or who willfully tried to hurt you requires a death of sorts. It means you are willing to lay down your right to be defended. Whom are you keeping in "prison" by refusing to offer forgiveness? By phone or by letter, why not say, "I forgive you. Will you forgive me for harboring unloving feelings toward you for so long?"

- In the cases of both Corrie ten Boom and Wayne Messmer, love overcame evil and suffering. But it also overcame thoughts of anger and resentment within the hearts of those who had been so deeply wronged. But that didn't happen overnight. Celebrate the freedom that is yours to openly admit whatever "unchristian" feelings you may have toward God or someone else. In your journal, candidly confess to the Lord feelings or doubts that you are struggling with. Ask him to change your heart. But start by admitting to what's in it.

- Christ's love compels us to live for others and not for ourselves, to serve selflessly. In what areas of your life are you continuing to live for yourself? How does that affect your ability to fulfill your God-given calling in life (see 2 Corinthians 5)?

- As you move on to incorporate the eight characteristics of heroic faith in your life, what evidence of love do you think God wants you to work on first? Willingness to lay down your life? Willingness to lay down your rights? Willingness to lay down your complaints? What steps will you take to do this?

Communion in the Sanctuary

Sanctuaries (by definition)
are a place of refuge. Right?
Not always.
In a world gone wrong
they are not exempt
from the Evil One's advances.
Chances are, many who gather in them
have lost a loved one
or have themselves been ambushed
and are bleeding.
Heeding Christ's warning
of promised persecution,
His Body collapses, exhausted.
But needing one another,
they hold each other

(and the cup and the bread).
They sing of heaven
and of a matchless weight of glory
that concludes each martyr's story
where in the end
all who persevere
live happily-ever-after.
Communion for these
is far more than an abstract ritual.
It is a vivid reminder that suffering and death
give way to hope and joy and eternal life
(not to mention a victor's crown).
Communion for them
is the safety they feel
while huddled in an unsafe place.

by Greg Asimakoupoulos